Applied Data Mining

Contents

Chapter 1

Able Danger

Able Danger was a classified military planning effort led by the U.S. Special Operations Command (SOCOM) and the Defense Intelligence Agency (DIA). It was created as a result of a directive from the Joint Chiefs of Staff in early October 1999 by Chairman of the Joint Chiefs of Staff Hugh Shelton, to develop an information operations campaign plan against transnational terrorism.

According to statements by Lt. Col. Anthony Shaffer and those of four others, Able Danger had identified 2 of 3 Al Qaeda cells active in the 9/11 attacks; the 'Brooklyn cell' linked to "Blind Sheik" Omar Abdel-Rahman, including September 11 attacks leader Mohamed Atta, and three of the 9/11 plot's other 19 hijackers.

In December 2006, a sixteen-month investigation by the US Senate Intelligence Committee concluded "Able Danger did not identify Mohamed Atta or any other 9/11 hijacker at any time prior to September 11, 2001," and dismissed other assertions that have fueled 9/11 conspiracy theories. The Senate Judiciary Committee first attempted to investigate the matter for the Senate in September, 2005. The Pentagon "ordered five key witnesses not to testify", according to Senate Judiciary Committee Chairman Arlen Specter. "That looks to me as if it may be obstruction of the committee's activities," Specter, R-Pennsylvania, said at the start of his committee's hearing into the unit.[1]

Attorney Mark Zaid, representing Lt. Colonel Anthony Shaffer and the other four Able Danger employees at the Senate Judiciary Committee hearing in September 2005, pointed out to the Committee that his clients had been forbidden by the Pentagon to testify to the Committee. He also discussed the Defense Intelligence Agency's decision to suspend Lt. Colonel Shaffer's security clearance shortly after it became known that he had provided information to the 9/11 Commission on Able Danger. "Based on years of experience I can say categorically that the basis for the revocation was questionable at best."[2] [3]

An investigation by the Defense Department Inspector General's office (IG) in September 2006 concluded that "the evidence did not support assertions that Able Danger identified the September 11, 2001, terrorists nearly a year before the attack, that Able Danger team members were prohibited from sharing information with law enforcement authorities, or that DoD officials acted against LTC Shaffer for his disclosures regarding Able Danger." However, some of the people questioned by the IG claimed their statements to the IG were distorted by investigators in the final IG's report, and the report omitted essential information that they had provided. Lt. Col Tony Shaffer has claimed that the DOD retaliated against him for speaking out publicly about the IG report's distortions.[4]

The Senate panel of investigators said there was no evidence DoD lawyers stopped analysts from sharing findings with the FBI before the attacks. Analysts had created charts that included pictures of then-known Al Qaeda operatives, but none including Atta. A follow-up chart made after the attacks did show Atta. The Senate Committee said its findings were consistent with those of the DoD inspector general, released in September 2006. [5] [6]

1.1   Overview

The program used data mining techniques to associate open source information with classified information in an attempt to make connections among individual members of terrorist groups as part of its original "intelligence preparation of the battlespace". The objective of this particular project was to ascertain whether the data mining techniques and open source material were effective tools in determining terrorist activities, and if the resultant data could be used to create operational plans that could be executed in a timely fashion to interrupt, capture and/or destroy terrorists or their cells.[7][8]

According to statements by Lt. Col. Anthony Shaffer and those of four others, Able Danger had identified 2 of 3 Al Qaeda cells active in the 9/11 attacks; the 'Brooklyn cell' linked to Blind Sheik Omar Abdel-Rahman, including September 11 attacks leader Mohamed Atta, and three of the 9/11 plot's other 19 hijackers, as possible members of an al Qaeda cell linked to the 1993 World Trade Center bombing.[9]

This theory was heavily investigated and researched by Republican Representative Curt Weldon, vice chairman of the House Armed Services and House Homeland Security committees. However, Defense Intelligence Agency leadership had already ordered the hurried destruction of mined data, source databases, charts & resultant documents on entirely spurious legal grounds. DIA also prevented key personnel from testifying to both the Senate Judiciary & Senate Intelligence Committees, though after numerous denials did admit the program's existence.[10]

In December 2006, an investigation by the US Senate Intelligence Committee concluded that assertions could not be confirmed. It stated that they were unable to find supporting evidence regarding "one of the most disturbing claims about the Sept. 11 terrorist strikes."[5] This report released by the Senate Intelligence Committee copied, nearly verbatim, the United States Department of Defense Inspector General's September 2006 report on Able Danger.

1.2   Assertion that Able Danger identified 9/11 hijackers

The existence of Able Danger, and its purported early identification of the 9/11 terrorists, was first disclosed publicly on June 19, 2005, in an article[11] by Keith Phucas, a reporter for *The Times Herald*, a Norristown, Pennsylvania, daily newspaper. Eight days later, on June 27, 2005, Representative Curt Weldon, vice chairman of the House Armed Services and House Homeland Security committees and the principal source for the Phucas article, gave a special orders speech on the House floor detailing Able Danger:

> Mr. Speaker, I rise because information has come to my attention over the past several months that is very disturbing. I have learned that, in fact, one of our Federal agencies had, in fact, identified the major New York cell of Mohamed Atta prior to 9/11; and I have learned, Mr. Speaker, that in September 2000, that Federal agency actually was prepared to bring the FBI in and prepared to work with the FBI to take down the cell that Mohamed Atta was involved in in New York City, along with two of the other terrorists. I have also learned, Mr. Speaker, that when that recommendation was discussed within that Federal agency, the lawyers in the administration at that time said, you cannot pursue contact with the FBI against that cell. Mohamed Atta is in the U.S. on a green card, and we are fearful of the fallout from the Waco incident. So we did not allow that Federal agency to proceed.[12]

Rep. Weldon later reiterated these concerns during news conferences on February 14, 2006. He believed that Able Danger identified Mohamed Atta 13 separate times prior to 9/11 and that the unit also identified a potential situation in Yemen two weeks prior to the October 12, 2000 attack on the USS *Cole*.[13] The Pentagon released a statement in response, stating that they wished to address these issues during a congressional hearing before a House Armed Services subcommittee scheduled for Wednesday, February 15, 2006.

1.2.1   Able Danger and the 9/11 Commission

Curt Weldon's assertion that Able Danger identified the 9/11 hijackers was picked up by the national media in August 2005, after it was reported in the bimonthly *Government Security News*.[14] In addition to asserting that Able Danger identified the 9/11 hijackers and was prevented from passing that information onto the FBI, Weldon also alleged the intelligence concerning Able Danger was provided to the 9/11 Commission and ignored.[15] Two 9/11 Commission members, Timothy J. Roemer and John F. Lehman, both claimed not to have received any information on Able Danger.[14]

Following the *GSN* report, members of the 9/11 Commission began commenting on the information they had on Able Danger and Atta. Lee H. Hamilton, former Vice Chair of the 9/11 Commission, and Al Felzenberg, a former spokesman for the 9/11 Commission,[16] both denied that the 9/11 Commission had any information on the identification of Mohamed Atta prior to the attacks.[17] Hamilton told the media, "The Sept. 11 commission did not learn of any U.S. government knowledge prior to 9/11 of surveillance of Mohamed Atta or of his cell.... Had we learned of it obviously it would've been a major focus of our investigation."[18]

On August 12, 2005, Hamilton and former 9/11 Commission chairman Thomas Kean issued a statement in response to media inquiries about the Commission's investigation of the Able Danger program.[19] It stated the Commission had been aware of the Able Danger program, and requested and obtained information about it from the Department of Defense, but none of the information provided had indicated the program had identified Atta or other 9/11 hijackers. They further stated that a claim about Atta having been identified prior to the attacks had been made to the 9/11 Commission on July 12, 2004 (just days before the Commission's report was released), by a United States Navy officer employed at DOD, but that

> The interviewee had no documentary evidence and said he had only seen the document briefly some years earlier. He could not describe what information had led to this supposed Atta identification. Nor could the interviewee recall, when questioned, any details about how he thought a link to Atta could have been made by this DOD program in 2000 or any time before 9/11. The Department of Defense documents had mentioned nothing about Atta, nor had anyone come forward between September 2001 and July 2004 with any similar information. Weighing this with the information about Atta's actual activities, the negligible information available about Atta to other U.S. government agencies and the German government before 9/11, and the interviewer's assessment of the interviewee's knowledge and credibility, the Commission staff concluded that the officer's account was not sufficiently reliable to warrant revision of the report or further investigation.[19]

Congressman Curt Weldon issued a response to the 9/11 Commission[20] clarifying the mission of Able Danger, expressing concern over the statements made by various members of the 9/11 Commission, and promising to push forward until it is understood why the DoD was unable to pass the information uncovered by Able Danger to the FBI, and why the 9/11 Commission failed to follow up on the information they were given on Able Danger.

> The 9/11 Commission has released multiple statements over the past week, each of which has significantly changed – from initially denying ever being briefed to acknowledging being briefed on both operation ABLE DANGER and Mohamed Atta. The information was omitted primarily because they found it to be suspect despite having been briefed on it two times by two different military officers on active duty. Additionally, the 9/11 Commission also received documents from the Department of Defense on ABLE DANGER.[20]

Congressman Weldon reiterated these statements in testimony before the Senate Judiciary Committee on September 21, 2005.[21]

1.2.2 Able Danger data destroyed

In his book *Countdown to Terror*, Weldon asserted that an Able Danger chart produced in 1999 identifying 9/11 hijackers Mohamed Atta, Marwan al-Shehhi, Khalid al-Mihdhar and Nawaf al-Hazmi had been presented to then-Deputy National Security Advisor Jim Steinberg. Weldon went on to claim that he had personally presented the chart to then-Deputy National Security Advisor Stephen Hadley in 2001, days after the 9/11 attacks.[22]

He later stated that he was no longer sure that Atta's name appeared on that document.[23]

Congressman Peter Hoekstra, who was then chairman of the House Intelligence Committee, investigated the matter at Weldon's request, was reported to have cautioned against "hyperventilating" before the completion of a "thorough" probe. Pentagon officials said they were unaware that any Able Danger material named Atta. They declined to comment on the reports as they worked to clarify the matter.[23]

On August 14, 2005, Mike Kelly, a columnist for *The (Bergen) Record* (New Jersey), described a telephone interview, arranged by the staff of Rep. Curt Weldon, with a man who identified himself as a member of the Able Danger team, but asked that his name not be revealed. In the interview, the man claimed his team had identified Mohamed Atta and three other 9/11 hijackers as likely Al-Qaeda terrorists operating in the United States, but were prevented from passing this information on to the FBI by government lawyers. He also claimed he was ignored by the 9/11 Commission's staff when he approached them on two occasions to explain Able Danger's work.[24]

On September 15, 2005, Weldon asserted that he had identified an employee who had been ordered to destroy the 2.5 terabytes (TB) of data collected by Able Danger two years before the 9/11 attack.[25]

1.3   Weldon changes his story

A *Time* magazine article dated August 14, 2005, reports that Weldon admitted he is no longer sure that Atta's name was on the chart he presented to Hadley and that he was unable to verify whether this was the case, having handed over his only copy, and that a reconstruction was used for post-9/11 presentations.[26] Weldon gave a talk at the Heritage Foundation with a chart he described as the one handed over on May 23, 2002. However, a week later he referred reporters to a recently reconstructed version of the chart in his office where, among dozens of names and photos of terrorists from around the world, there was a color mug shot of Mohammad Atta, circled in black marker.

1.4   Comments by members of the Able Danger team

1.4.1   Lt. Col. Anthony Shaffer

After Weldon's assertions were disputed, Lt. Col. Anthony Shaffer, a member of the Able Danger team, identified himself as Weldon's source. Shaffer claimed that he alerted the FBI in September 2000 about the information uncovered by the secret military unit "Able Danger," but he alleges three meetings he set up with bureau officials were blocked by military lawyers. Shaffer, who at the time worked for the Defense Intelligence Agency, claims he communicated to members of the 9/11 Commission that Able Danger had identified two of the three cells responsible for 9/11 prior to the attacks, but the Commission did not include this information in their final report.[27]

Shaffer specifically states that in Jan 2000, Able Danger data-mining revealed the existence of a 'Brooklyn' Al-Qaeda cell connected to the "Blind Sheik" Omar Abdel-Rahman, as well as two other cells overseas. Shaffer & Philpott examined this chart of Al Qaeda suspected operatives, containing names & photos, and Philpott pointed out one particular sinister and "scary looking dude" -- Mohammed Atta.[9]

Shaffer's lawyer, Mark Zaid, has revealed that Shaffer had been placed on paid administrative leave for what he called "petty and frivolous" reasons and had his security clearance suspended in March 2004, following a dispute over travel mileage expenses and personal use of a work cell phone.[28] These allegations are claimed to have been pursued in bad faith & breach of process, in relation for Shaffer talking to the 9/11 Commission. Army investigations subsequently found these to be ill-grounded, and cleared his promotion.

As Lt. Col. Shaffer received a memorandum of OPCON status from Joint Task Force (JTF) 121, confirming his attachment to this element 1 November through 1 December 2004, and participating in the 75th Ranger Regiment's nighttime air assault of 11 November 2003, the controversy of his wearing the 75th Ranger Regiment patch as his "combat patch" is closed in his favor. In the Army Reserve, Lt. Col. Shaffer is now assigned as the G6 of the 94th Division (Prov), Ft. Lee, VA.

Congressman Weldon asked for a new probe into the activities undertaken to silence Lt. Col. Shaffer from publicly commenting on Able Danger and Able Danger's identification of the 9/11 hijackers. Weldon called the activities "a deliberate campaign of character assassination."[29]

Shaffer has also told the story of Central Intelligence Agency (CIA) opposition to Able Danger, prior to 9/11, based on the view that Able Danger was encroaching on CIA turf. According to Shaffer, the CIA representative said, "I clearly understand. We're going after the leadership. You guys are going after the body. But, it doesn't matter. The bottom line is, CIA will never give you the best information from "Alex Base" or anywhere else. CIA will never provide that to you because if you were successful in your effort to target Al Qaeda, you will steal our thunder. Therefore, we will not support this."[30]

1.4.2 Navy Captain Scott Phillpott

Capt. Scott Phillpott confirmed Shaffer's claims. "I will not discuss this outside of my chain of command," Phillpott said in a statement to Fox News. "I have briefed the Department of the Army, the Special Operations Command and the office of (Undersecretary of Defense for Intelligence) Dr. Cambone as well as the 9/11 Commission.[31] My story has remained consistent. Atta was identified by Able Danger in January/February 2000," he was quoted as saying.[32]

1.4.3 James D. Smith

Shaffer's claims were also confirmed by James D. Smith, a civilian contractor who worked on Able Danger. In an interview with Fox News, Smith reported that the project had involved analysis of data from a large number of public sources and 20 to 30 individuals.[33]

Smith stated that Atta's name had emerged during an examination of individuals known to have ties to Omar Abdel Rahman, a leading figure in the first World Trade Center bombing.

1.4.4 Major Eric Kleinsmith

Major Eric Kleinsmith, who was with the Army and chief of intelligence for LIWA until February 2001, testified that he was ordered to destroy Able Danger's information. "I deleted the data," he said. "There were two sets, classified and unclassified, and also an 'all sorts,'" which contained a blend of the two, "plus charts we'd produced." Kleinsmith deleted the 2.5 terabytes of data in May and June, 2000, on orders of Tony Gentry, general counsel of the Army Intelligence and Security Command.[34]

1.4.5 Other witnesses

The Defense Department announced its findings on September 1, 2005, after a three-week investigation into Able Danger. The statement announced the discovery of three other witnesses in addition to Shaffer and Phillpott who confirm Able Danger had produced a chart that "either mentioned Atta by name as an al-Qaeda operative [and/or] showed his photograph." Four of the five witnesses remember the photo on the chart. The fifth remembers only Atta being cited by name. The Pentagon describes the witnesses as "credible" but stated that the document which allegedly mentioned Atta could not be found.[35][36]

1.5 The wall

Former chief assistant U.S. attorney Andrew McCarthy and others have asserted that the Able Danger intelligence was suppressed as a result of a policy of forbidding the CIA and FBI to share intelligence known as "the wall."[37] During the 9/11 Commission hearings, then-Attorney General John Ashcroft testified the wall was strengthened under the Clinton administration by Jamie Gorelick to prohibit sharing of terrorist intelligence within the federal government.[38]

This assertion was disputed by former senator Slade Gorton (R-WA), a member of the 9-11 Commission, who said, "nothing Jamie Gorelick wrote had the slightest impact on the Department of Defense or its willingness or ability to share intelligence information with other intelligence agencies." Gorton also asserted that "the wall" was a long-standing policy that had resulted from the Church Committee in the 1970s, and that the policy only prohibits transfer of certain information *from* prosecutors *to* the intelligence services and never prohibited information flowing in the opposite direction.

1.6   Skepticism

1.6.1   Two Attas theory

Mickey Kaus of Slate.com, referring to Tom Maguire's "Two Attas" theory,[39] speculates that "the 'Atta' fingered by Able Danger was really the first, 'Abu Nidal' Atta, and not the second, 9/11 'Al Qaeda' Atta," and that this may help explain this Able Danger issue.[40] Snopes.com clarified a widely circulated email that claimed the two Attas were one and the same.[41]

Another variation of the Two Attas theory reported by Kaus notes that Omar Abdel Rahman also had an associate with the name Mohamed El-Amir (a name sometimes used by Atta) who was not the Mohamed Atta involved in the 9/11 hijacking.[42]

However, Shaffer clarified that. He told 9/11 Commission staffers Able Danger identified three of the individuals in the terrorist cells that conducted the 9/11 attacks, to include Atta - Shaffer did not mention the names of any other of the 9/11 hijackers in his disclosure to the 9/11 staff. A fourth 9/11 terrorist came from the second cell.[43] Eric Umansky states the problem this way: "In fact, the two-Atta theory only leaves one major issue unexplained: What about the three other 9/11 hijackers that Able Danger purportedly fingered?

The Department of Defense released a report addressing the issue of two possible individuals with the last name of Atta and explaining that it was basically a clerical error.

> When we reviewed INS records, they appeared to reflect two entries by Atta into the United States on January 10, 2001, which initially raised a question as to whether Atta had entered twice on the same day or whether a second person posing as Atta also entered on January 10, 2001. The NIIS printout for the first entry reflects that Atta entered with an admission period of January 10, 2001, to September 8, 2001 (admission number 68653985708). The second record reflects a second entry on January 10, 2001, with an admission period from January 10, 2001, to July 9, 2001 (admission number 10847166009). However, this occurred because the inspector at the Miami District Office who changed Atta's admission date failed to follow the proper procedure to ensure that the previous entry would be corrected, and a new entry was created in NIIS. The inspector sent the old I-94 and the corrected I-94 to the contractor which data enters I-94s for the INS. The May 2, 2001, transaction with Atta was data entered and then uploaded to NIIS as if it were a new entry by Atta. This happened because the inspector issued a new I-94 with a new admission number on it. To prevent two entries from occurring in NIIS, the inspector should have crossed out the admission number on the new I-94, made a reference to the previous admission number and noted that it was not a new entry.[44]

It should be noted that IG report is disputed by Lt. Col. Shaffer and other Able Danger team members, some of whom were never interviewed by the IG's office nor the 9/11 commission. Congressman Weldon also claims the report was a hurried, botched up investigation that was intended to close the books on the subject rather than report on the facts.

For example this lead was never followed: "Normen Pentolino, operations manager at the Hollywood store, said two cashiers told FBI agents they might have recognized Atta, but weren't certain. Sources inside the store said Atta may have held a BJ's membership card for more than two years."[45]

1.6.2   Timing

Kevin Drum, writing for *The Washington Monthly* notes that reports of the precise date at which the information was allegedly passed to the FBI vary considerably. It is most unlikely that Able Danger would have identified a terrorist called "Mohamed Atta" before May 2000.

> Since 9/11, of course, we have retrieved every scrap of information ever known about Mohamed Atta, so we know what information would have been available to the Able Danger data mining operation. And what we know is that Mohamed Atta sent his first email to friends in the U.S. in March 2000 and received his first U.S. visa on May 18, 2000. Moreover, that was the first time he had ever gone by the name "Mohamed Atta." His full name is "Mohamed Mohamed el-Amir Awad el-Sayed Atta," and prior to 2000 he went by "Mohamed el-Amir."

1.6.3 Documentation

The Able Danger computer records were erased. To date, no electronic or paper document has shown that any connection was made to Atta *before* 9/11. No emails to or from the Able Danger team make any references to Atta, nor do any paper documents between the team and any other DoD teams or offices. No notes taken at any pre 9/11 meetings between the DoD and FBI, or interoffice DoD meetings, show any mention of Atta or a terrorist cell in New York.

1.7 Congressional hearings

Senate Judiciary Committee Chairman Arlen Specter held a hearing on September 21, 2005, looking into the facts about Able Danger. However, Lt. Col. Shaffer and the other four members of Able Danger were ordered not to testify by the Department of Defense.[46] Senator Specter decided to go forward with the hearings anyway.

Senator Specter wondered if the Posse Comitatus Act may have been the reason Defense Department attorneys would not allow Able Danger to turn over information to the FBI. The Posse Comitatus Act prevents the military from being engaged in law enforcement activities, including gathering information on U.S. persons, despite the aliens were not specifically United States citizens. Speaking on behalf of Lt. Col. Shaffer, attorney Mark Zaid testified "Those within Able Danger were confident they weren't compiling information on US persons. They were potentially people connected to US persons."[47]

Zaid also strongly asserted on behalf of his clients,

> "Let me emphasize two specific items for clarification purposes because they have been distorted and invited undue criticism from some.
> At no time did Able Danger identify Mohamed Atta as being physically present in the United States.
> No information obtained at the time would have led anyone to believe criminal activity had taken place or that any specific terrorist activities were being planned. Again, the identification of the four 9/11 hijackers was simply through associational activities. Those associations could have been completely innocuous or nefarious. It was impossible to tell which, and the unclassified work of Able Danger was not designed to address that question."[46]

He further added that

> "unfortunately we are not aware of the continuing existence of any chart containing Mohamed Atta's name or photograph. The copies that would have been in the possession of the U.S. Army were apparently destroyed by March 2001. The copies within Lt Col Shaffer's files were destroyed by the DIA in approximately Spring 2004. The destruction of these files is an important element to this story and I encourage the Committee to investigate it further. It would appear, particularly given the Defense Department's outright refusal to allow those involved with Able Danger to testify today, that an obstructionist attitude exists. The question for this Committee is to investigate how far that position extends and why."[48]

Former Army Major Erik Kleinsmith, former head of the Pentagon's Land Warfare Analysis Department, testified at the hearing that he had been instructed to destroy data and documents related to Able Danger in May and June 2000. When asked whether the information could have prevented the attack on September 11 of 2001, he answered that he would not speculate to that, but that the information might have been useful.[49]

1.8 Subsequent investigations

On February 14, 2006, Congressmen Curt Weldon charged that contrary to testimony, not all the data on Able Danger had been destroyed. Weldon claimed to be in contact with people in the government still able to do data-mining who got 13 hits on Mohamed Atta. Weldon also claimed that Able Danger information was found in Pentagon files as recently as two weeks prior to his statement and that a general was present when the files were taken from the cabinet.[50] The next day, there was a joint committee meeting with the Subcommittee on Terrorism, Unconventional Threats and Capabilities and the Subcommittee on Strategic Forces, to discuss the Able Danger program.[51]

On September 21, 2006, *The Washington Post* reported that a Defense Department investigation into Able Danger found that Able Danger did not identify Mohamed Atta or any other hijacker before the September 11 attacks, and that a widely discussed chart was "a sample document passed to the military as an example of how to organize large amounts of data," and was created after 9/11.

1.8.1   Inspector General's report

On September 18, 2006, the Office of the Deputy Inspector General for Investigations released a report stating that Shaffer was put on leave, that the crew responsible for removing any classified documents from his office to prevent his taking them home with him found that he did not have any of the Able Danger-related documents trusted to him he claimed he had,[52] and that despite the fact that the Army cleared him of any wrongdoing in the allegations "DIA officials would have taken action to revoke LTC Shaffer's access and clearance regardless of his disclosures to the DIA IG, the 9/11 Commission staff members, Members of Congress, or the media.[53]

The Department of Defense investigation concluded:

- The anti-terrorist program, Able Danger, did not identify Mohamed Atta or any other 9/11 terrorists before the 9/11 attack.

- Able Danger members were not prohibited from sharing intelligence information with law enforcement authorities or other agencies that could have acted on that information. In fact, Able Danger produced no actionable intelligence information.

- The destruction of Able Danger documentation at LIWA and Garland was appropriate and complied with applicable DoD regulations.

- The Able Danger program was not terminated prematurely. It concluded after it had achieved its objective and its work products were used in follow-on intelligence gathering efforts at USSOCOM."[54]

Alleged evidence of IG cover-up

Five witnesses who had worked on Able Danger and had been questioned by the Defense Department's Inspector General later told investigative journalists that their statements to the IG were distorted by investigators in the final IG's report, or the report omitted essential information that they had provided. The alleged distortions of the IG report centered around excluding any evidence that Able Danger had identified and tracked Atta years before 9/11. The witnesses reported to the journalists that the IG investigators got increasingly hostile in an effort to intimidate the witnesses into changing their testimony to drop any assertion that they had identified and tracked Atta, and this suggests a cover-up by the IG of Able Danger's findings. Witnesses reported telling Philip Zelikow, executive director of the 9/11 Commission, that Able Danger had identified Atta well before the 9/11 attacks, but Zelikow showed no interest in their testimony. Lt. Col Tony Shaffer also reported that the DOD has retaliated against him for speaking out publicly about the IG report's distortions.[4]

1.9   Movie

The independent film, *Able Danger* was released in 2008. The screenplay written by Paul Krik centers around a Brooklyn, New York coffee shop owner who receives a disk proving a tie between the CIA and the 9/11 attacks.[55]

1.10 Book

Operation Dark Heart by Anthony A. Shaffer, released in September 2010,[56] includes memories of his time reporting to the 9/11 commission about Able Danger's findings. The 10,000 copies of the books have not been released yet. The DOD's Defense Intelligence Agency reviewers identified more than 200 passages suspected of containing classified information.[57] "Specifically, the DIA wanted references to a meeting between Lt. Col. Tony Shaffer, the book's author, and the executive director of the 9/11 Commission, Philip Zelikow, removed".[58] DOD took the highly unusual step of purchasing all available copies of Shaffer's book at a cost of $47,000 and destroying them to deny the public the ability to read the book.[4]

1.11 See also

- 9/11 commission report

- Criticisms of the 9/11 Commission Report

- September 11, 2001 attacks

- Bin Laden Issue Station (The CIA's bin Laden tracking unit, 1996–2005)

- War games in progress on September 11, 2001

- Collapse of the World Trade Center

- 9/11 conspiracy theories

1.12 References

[1] "Specter: Pentagon may be obstructing committee". Washington: cnn.com. 21 September 2005. Retrieved April 26, 2010. That looks to me as it may be obstruction of the committee's activities.

[2] zaid, mark (21 September 2005). "prepared statement of mark s. zaid, esq., before the committee on judiciary, united states senate". washington, d.c.: committee on judiciary, united states senate. Archived from the original on 11 April 2010. Retrieved April 26, 2010. Based on years of experience I can say categorically that the basis for the revocation was questionable at best.

[3] Senate Select Committee on Intelligence (22 December 2006). "ssci #2006-4735" (PDF). washington, d.c. p. 9. Archived (PDF) from the original on 7 May 2010. Retrieved April 26, 2010.

[4] Fox News, 2010 Oct. 4, "Exclusive: Witnesses in Defense Dept. Report Suggest Cover-Up of 9/11 Findings," http://www.foxnews.com/politics/2010/10/04/exclusive-witnesses-defense-department-report-suggest-cover-findings/

[5] Miller, Greg (2006-12-25). "Alarming 9/11 Claim Is Baseless, Panel Says". Los Angeles Times. Retrieved 2010-01-10.

[6] Anne Flaherty (2006-12-26). "Senators Nix Pre-9/11 Hijacker ID Theory". *The Washington Post*. Associated Press. Retrieved 2008-11-21.

[7] An example of a chart produced as output by the project's data mining and visualization suite is called the 3.21.00 Chart. (DIAC Link Chart declassified 3.21.00, produced on March 21, 2000, and reproduced on author Peter Lance's website for his book Triple Cross Another barely readable sample chart was published by the Defense Department's Inspector General's Office on page 14 of the Able Danger Investigation Report.

[8] Patience Wait has reported that a follow-on project appears to have been funded and implemented by the Intelligence Community and was originally named Able Providence. Data Mining Offensive in the Works - Patience Wait - GCN Magazine, 10/10/2005

[9] Shaffer, Anthony (2010). *Operation Dark Heart*. St Martin's Press. p. 170. ISBN 978-0-312-60369-4.

[10] Shaffer, Anthony (2010). *Operation Dark Heart*. St Martin's Press. pp. 274–275. ISBN 978-0-312-60369-4.

[11] Phucas, Keith (19 June 2005). "Missed chance on way to 9/11". *The Times Herald* (Shelley Meenan). Retrieved 2006-08-03.

[12] United States Congress. "U.S. Intelligence. PDF" *Congressional Record—House*. Washington, D.C.: GPO, 27 June 2005. 109th Cong., 1st sess. HR H5244.

[13] Hefling, Kimberly (2006-02-14). "Weldon: 'Able Danger' ID'd 9/ll Ringleader". Associated Press. Archived from the original on 2007-11-10. Retrieved 2010-01-11.

[14] Goodwin, Jacob (August 2005). "Did DoD lawyers blow the chance to nab Atta?". *GSN: Government Security News* (Edward Tyler). Archived from the original on 2007-09-15. Retrieved 2010-01-10.

[15] United States Congress. "U.S. Intelligence. PDF" *Congressional Record—House*. Washington, D.C.: GPO, 27 June 2005. 109th Cong., 1st sess. HR H5250. Retrieved on 2006-08-03.

[16] Andrews, Wyatt; The Associated Press (9 August 2005). "New Pre-9/11 Intel Questions". *Special Report: War on Terror* (CBS News). Retrieved 2006-08-03.

[17] Douglas Jehl; Philip Shenon; Eric Schmitt (8 August 2005). "Four in 9/11 Plot Are Called Tied to Qaeda in '00". New York Times. Retrieved 2006-08-03. More than a year before the Sept. 11 attacks, a small, highly classified military intelligence unit identified Mohamed Atta and three other future hijackers as likely members of a cell of Al Qaeda operating in the United States, according to a former defense intelligence official and a Republican member of Congress.

[18] Herridge, Catherine; Liza Porteus; The Associated Press (11 August 2005). "Source: 9/11 Panel Staffers Probing Documents on 'Able Danger'". *Fox News Politics* (Fox News Channel). Archived from the original on 5 September 2006. Retrieved 2006-08-03.

[19] Kean, Thomas; Hamilton, Lee H. (2005-08-12). "Kean-Hamilton Statement on Able Danger" (PDF) (Press release).

[20] Curt Weldon (2005-08-12). "Weldon Responds to Omission of ABLE DANGER From 9/11 Report" (Press release). 9/11 Citizens Watch.

[21] "Honorable Curt Weldon's testimony at Able Danger and Intelligence Information Sharing". Federation of American Scientists website.

[22] Curt Weldon (2005-07-25). *Countdown to Terror: The Top Secret Information that Could Prevent the Next Terrorist Attack on America...And How the CIA has Ignored it*. Regnery Publishing. ISBN 978-0-89526-005-5.

[23] Bennett, Brian; Timothy J. Burger; Douglas Waller (2005-08-14). "Was Mohamed Atta Overlooked?". *Time* (Time Warner). Retrieved 2006-08-17.

[24] Kelly, Mike (2005-08-14). "Deadly tale of incompetence". *The Record (Bergen Co., NJ)* (North Jersey Media Group). Archived from the original on June 13, 2006. Retrieved 2006-08-17.

[25] De, Donna (2005-09-16). "Weldon: Atta Papers Destroyed on Orders". Associated Press. Archived from the original on 2005-09-22. Retrieved 2010-01-10.

[26] Bennett, Brian; Burger, Timothy J.; Waller, Douglas (2005-08-14). "Was Mohamed Atta Overlooked?". Time Magazine.

[27] "The Situation Room Transcript". CNN. 2005-08-17.

[28] "Pentagon Investigates Able Danger Work". Fox News. 2005-08-18.

[29] "Congressman wants new Able Danger probe". United Press International. 2005-10-19. Archived from the original on 2005-12-28. Retrieved 2010-01-10.

[30] Goodwin, Jacob (September 2005). "Inside Able Danger – The Secret Birth, Extraordinary Life and Untimely Death of a U.S. Military Intelligence Program". *GSN: Government Security News*. World Business Media, LLC. Archived from the original on 2005-09-24. Retrieved 2010-05-22.

[31] *Memorandum of Scott Phillpott statement to the 9-11 Commission* (PDF), Cryptome, 2004-07-13

[32] "Navy Captain Backs Able Danger Claims". Fox News. 2005-08-23.

[33] "Third Source Backs 'Able Danger' Claims About Atta". Fox News. 2005-08-28.

[34] Patience Wait (2005-10-07). "Data-mining offensive in the works". Government Computer News. Retrieved 2010-01-11.

[35] Shanker, Thom (September 2, 2005). "Terrorist Known Before 9/11, More Say". *New York Times*. Retrieved 11 June 2015.

[36] Wood, Sgt. Sara (September 1, 2005). "DoD Discusses Able Danger Findings". *American Forces Press Service* (United States Department of Defense). Retrieved 2010-05-22.

[37] Andrew C. McCarthy (2004-04-19). "The Wall Truth". National Review Online.

[38] "Instructions on Separation of Certain Foreign CounterIntelligence and Criminal Investigations" (PDF). US Department of Justice website. Retrieved 2008-12-28.

[39] "Able Danger - Muddying The Waters". Just One Minute Blog. 2005-08-18.

[40] Mickey Kaus (2005-08-21). "The "Two Atta" Theory". Slate.com.

[41] "Atta Boy". Snopes.com.

[42] Mickey Kaus (2005-08-29). "Able Danger Mystery Solved?". Slate.com.

[43]

[44] "The Immigration and Naturalization Service's Contacts With Two September 11 Terrorists: A Review of the INS's Admissions of Mohamed Atta and Marwan Alshehhi, its Processing of their Change of Status Applications, and its Efforts to Track Foreign Students in the United States". Website of the United States Office of the Inspector General. 2002-05-20.

[45] Babson, Jennifer; Lebowitz, Larry; Viglucci, Andres (2001-09-18). "Broward library PCs yield clues". Miami Herald. Archived from the original on 2001-10-21.

[46] "Specter: Pentagon may be obstructing committee". CNN. 2005-09-21.

[47] "Transcript of The Able Danger Senate Hearings". PBS. 2005-09-21.

[48] "Prepared Statement of Mark S. Zaid, Esq. Before the Committee on Judiciary, United States Senate" (PDF). Federation of American Scientists Website. 2005-09-21. Retrieved 2008-12-28.

[49] "'Able Danger' Will Get Second Hearing". Fox News. 2005-09-24.

[50] Gossett, Sherrie (2006-02-15). "'Able Danger' Identified 9/11 Hijacker 13 Times". Cybercast News Service. Archived from the original on 2006-06-15. Retrieved 2010-01-10.

[51] "Joint Hearing on the Able Danger Program" (PDF) (Press release). The Federation of American Scientists website. 2006-02-15.

[52] Alleged Misconduct by Senior DOD Officials Concerning the Able Danger Program and Lieutenant Colonel Anthony A. Shaffer, US Army Reserve (PDF) (Report). p. 10. Retrieved 2008-12-28.

[53] Alleged Misconduct by Senior DOD Officials Concerning the Able Danger Program and Lieutenant Colonel Anthony A. Shaffer, US Army Reserve (PDF) (Report). p. 11. Retrieved 2008-12-28.

[54] Alleged Misconduct by Senior DOD Officials Concerning the Able Danger Program and Lieutenant Colonel Anthony A. Shaffer, US Army Reserve (PDF) (Report). p. 69. Retrieved 2008-12-28.

[55] Review by the Los Angeles Times October 31, 2008

[56] Shane, Scott (2010-09-10). "Pentagon Plan: Buying Books to Keep Secrets". *New York Times*. p. A16. Archived from the original on 2012-04-19. Retrieved 2012-04-19.

[57] NYT September 10, 2010

[58] Fox News September 10, 2010

Chapter 2

Anomaly Detection at Multiple Scales

Anomaly Detection at Multiple Scales, or **ADAMS**, is a $35 million DARPA project designed to identify patterns and anomalies in very large data sets. It is under DARPA's Information Innovation office and began in 2011.[1][2][3][4]

The project is intended to detect and prevent insider threats such as "a soldier in good mental health becoming homicidal or suicidal", an "innocent insider becoming malicious", or "a government employee [whom] abuses access privileges to share classified information".[2][5] Specific cases mentioned are Nidal Malik Hasan and Wikileaks alleged source Chelsea Manning.[6] Commercial applications may include finance.[6] The intended recipients of the system output are operators in the counterintelligence agencies.[2][5]

The Proactive Discovery of Insider Threats Using Graph Analysis and Learning is part of the ADAMS project.[5][7] The Georgia Tech team includes noted high-performance computing researcher David A. Bader.[8]

2.1   See also

- Cyber Insider Threat
- Einstein (US-CERT program)
- Threat (computer)
- Intrusion detection

2.2   References

[1] "ADAMS". DARPA Information Innovation Office. Retrieved 2011-12-05.

[2] "Anomaly Detection at Multiple Scales (ADAMS) Broad Agency Announcement DARPA-BAA-11-04" (PDF). General Services Administration. 2010-10-22. Retrieved 2011-12-05.

[3] Ackerman, Spencer (2010-10-11). "Darpa Starts Sleuthing Out Disloyal Troops". *Wired*. Retrieved 2011-12-06.

[4] Keyes, Charley (2010-10-27). "Military wants to scan communications to find internal threats". *CNN*. Retrieved 2011-12-06.

[5] "Georgia Tech Helps to Develop System That Will Detect Insider Threats from Massive Data Sets". Georgia Institute of Technology. 2011-11-10. Retrieved 2011-12-06.

[6] "Video Interview: DARPA's ADAMS Project Taps Big Data to Find the Breaking Bad". Inside HPC. 2011-11-29. Retrieved 2011-12-06.

[7] Brandon, John (2011-12-03). "Could the U.S. Government Start Reading Your Emails?". Fox News. Retrieved 2011-12-06.

[8] "Anomaly Detection at Multiple Scales". Georgia Tech College of Computing. Retrieved 2011-12-06.

Chapter 3

Behavioral analytics

Not to be confused with Applied Behavior Analysis.

Behavioral Analytics is a subset of business analytics that focuses on how and why users of eCommerce platforms, online games, & web applications behave. While business analytics has a more broad focus on the who, what, where and when of business intelligence, behavioral analytics narrows that scope, allowing one to take seemingly unrelated data points in order to extrapolate, predict and determine errors and future trends. It takes a more holistic and human view of data, connecting individual data points to tell us not only what is happening, but also how and why it is happening.

Behavioral analytics utilizes user data captured while the web application, game, or website is in use by analytic platforms like Google Analytics. Platform traffic data like navigation paths, clicks, social media interactions, purchasing decisions and marketing responsiveness is all recorded. Also, other more specific advertising metrics like click-to-conversion time, and comparisons between other metrics like the monetary value of an order and the amount of time spent on the site.[1] These data points are then compiled and analyzed, whether by looking at the timeline progression from when a user first entered the platform until a sale was made, or what other products a user bought or looked at before this purchase. Behavioral analysis allows future actions and trends to be predicted based on all the data collected.

3.1 Examples and real world applications

Data shows that a large percentage of users using a certain eCommerce platform found it by searching for "Thai food" on Google. After landing on the homepage, most people spent some time on the "Asian Food" page and then logged off without placing an order. Looking at each of these events as separate data points does not represent what is really going on and why people did not make a purchase. However, viewing these data points as a representation of overall user behavior enables one to interpolate how and why users acted in this particular case.

Behavioral analytics looks at all site traffic and page views as a timeline of connected events that did not lead to orders. Since most users left after viewing the "Asian Food" page, there could be a disconnect between what they are searching for on Google and what the "Asian Food" page displays. Knowing this, a quick look at the "Asian Food" page reveals that it does not display Thai food prominently and thus people do not think it is actually offered, even though it is.

Behavioral analytics is becoming increasingly popular in commercial environments. Amazon.com is a leader in using behavioral analytics to recommend additional products that customers are likely to buy based on their previous purchasing patterns on the site.[2] Behavioral analytics is also used by Target to suggest products to customers in their retail stores, while political campaigns use it to determine how potential voters should be approached.[3] In addition to retail and political applications, behavioral analytics is also used by banks and manufacturing firms to prioritize leads generated by their websites. Behavioral analytics also allow developers to manage users in online-gaming and web applications.[2]

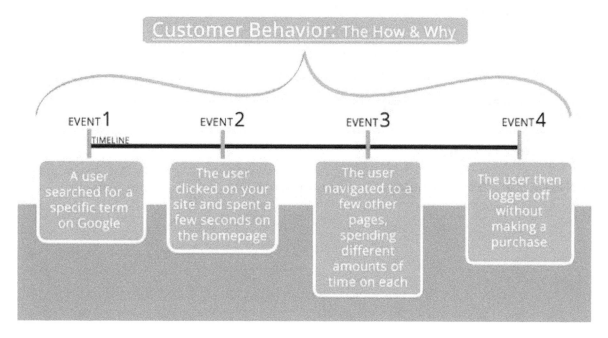

Visual Representation of Events that Make Up Behavioral Analysis

3.2   Types of Behavioral Analytics

- Ecommerce & Retail- Product recommendations and predicting future sales trends

- Online Gaming- Predicting usage trends, load, and user preferences in future releases

- Application Development- Determining how users use an application to predict future usage and preferences.

- Cohort Analysis- Breaking users down into similar groups to gain a more focused understanding of their behavior.

- Security - Detecting compromised credentials and insider threats by locating anomalous behavior.

3.3   See also

- Funnel analysis

- Path analysis

- Cohort analysis

- Big data

- Data mining

- Analytics

- Business Intelligence

- Test and Learn

- Business Process Discovery

- Statistics

- Customer dynamics

3.4 References

[1] Yamaguchi, Kohki. "Leveraging Advertising Data For Behavioral Insights". *Analytics & Marketing Column*. Marketing Land.

[2] "Oh behave! How behavioral analytics fuels more personalized marketing" (PDF). IBM Software. Retrieved 3 July 2013.

[3] Homa, Ken. "Behavioral analytics … bad when Target does it … OK for political campaigns?". *The Homa Files*.

3.5 Further reading

- Nagaitis, Mark. "Behavioral Analytics: The Why and How of E-Shopping". eCommerce Times.

Chapter 4

Business analytics

Not to be confused with Business analysis.

Business analytics (BA) refers to the skills, technologies, practices for continuous iterative exploration and investigation of past business performance to gain insight and drive business planning.[1] Business analytics focuses on developing new insights and understanding of business performance based on data and statistical methods. In contrast, business intelligence traditionally focuses on using a consistent set of metrics to both measure past performance and guide business planning, which is also based on data and statistical methods.

Business analytics makes extensive use of statistical analysis, including explanatory and predictive modeling,[2] and fact-based management to drive decision making. It is therefore closely related to management science. Analytics may be used as input for human decisions or may drive fully automated decisions. Business intelligence is querying, reporting, online analytical processing (OLAP), and "alerts."

In other words, querying, reporting, OLAP, and alert tools can answer questions such as what happened, how many, how often, where the problem is, and what actions are needed. Business analytics can answer questions like why is this happening, what if these trends continue, what will happen next (that is, predict), what is the best that can happen (that is, optimize).[3]

4.1 Examples of application

Banks, such as Capital One, use data analysis (or *analytics*, as it is also called in the business setting), to differentiate among customers based on credit risk, usage and other characteristics and then to match customer characteristics with appropriate product offerings. Harrah's, the gaming firm, uses analytics in its customer loyalty programs. E & J Gallo Winery quantitatively analyzes and predicts the appeal of its wines. Between 2002 and 2005, Deere & Company saved more than $1 billion by employing a new analytical tool to better optimize inventory.[3] Example : It can help you focus on the fundamental objectives of the business and the ways analytics can serve them. A telecoms company that pursues efficient call centre usage over customer service may save money.

4.2 Types of analytics

- Decisive analytics: supports human decisions with visual analytics the user models to reflect reasoning.[4]

- Descriptive Analytics: Gain insight from historical data with reporting, scorecards, clustering etc.

- Predictive analytics (predictive modeling using statistical and machine learning techniques)

- Prescriptive analytics recommend decisions using optimization, simulation etc.

4.3 Basic domains within analytics

- Behavioral analytics
- Cohort Analysis
- Collections analytics
- Contextual data modeling - supports the human reasoning that occurs after viewing "executive dashboards" or any other visual analytics
- Cyber analytics
- Financial services analytics
- Fraud analytics
- Marketing analytics
- Pricing analytics
- Retail sales analytics
- Risk & Credit analytics
- Supply Chain analytics
- Talent analytics
- Telecommunications
- Transportation analytics
- Anti-Crisis analytics[5]

4.4 History

Analytics have been used in business since the management exercises were put into place by Frederick Winslow Taylor in the late 19th century. Henry Ford measured the time of each component in his newly established assembly line. But analytics began to command more attention in the late 1960s when computers were used in decision support systems. Since then, analytics have changed and formed with the development of enterprise resource planning (ERP) systems, data warehouses, and a large number of other software tools and processes.[3]

In later years the business analytics have exploded with the introduction to computers. This change has brought analytics to a whole new level and has made the possibilities endless. As far as analytics has come in history, and what the current field of analytics is today many people would never think that analytics started in the early 1900s with Mr. Ford himself.

4.5 Challenges

Business analytics depends on sufficient volumes of high quality data. The difficulty in ensuring data quality is integrating and reconciling data across different systems, and then deciding what subsets of data to make available.[3]

Previously, analytics was considered a type of after-the-fact method of forecasting consumer behavior by examining the number of units sold in the last quarter or the last year. This type of data warehousing required a lot more storage space than it did speed. Now business analytics is becoming a tool that can influence the outcome of customer interactions.[6] When a specific customer type is considering a purchase, an analytics-enabled enterprise can modify the sales pitch to appeal to that consumer. This means the storage space for all that data must react extremely fast to provide the necessary data in real-time.

4.6 Competing on analytics

Thomas Davenport, professor of information technology and management at Babson College argues that businesses can optimize a distinct business capability via analytics and thus better compete. He identifies these characteristics of an organization that are apt to compete on analytics:[3]

- One or more senior executives who strongly advocate fact-based decision making and, specifically, analytics

- Widespread use of not only descriptive statistics, but also predictive modeling and complex optimization techniques

- Substantial use of analytics across multiple business functions or processes

- Movement toward an enterprise level approach to managing analytical tools, data, and organizational skills and capabilities

4.7 See also

- Analytics

- Business analysis

- Business analyst

- Business intelligence

- Business process discovery

- Customer dynamics

- Data mining

- OLAP

- Statistics

- Test and learn

4.8 References

[1] Beller, Michael J.; Alan Barnett (2009-06-18). "Next Generation Business Analytics". Lightship Partners LLC. Retrieved 2009-06-20.

[2] Galit Schmueli and Otto Koppius. "Predictive vs. Explanatory Modeling in IS Research" (PDF).

[3] Davenport, Thomas H.; Harris, Jeanne G. (2007). *Competing on analytics : the new science of winning*. Boston, Mass.: Harvard Business School Press. ISBN 978-1-4221-0332-6.

[4] "Analytics List". Retrieved 3 April 2015.

[5] Kuandykov, Lev (2015). *Anti-Crisis Analytics: Business Analytics That Helps Before, During, and After a Crisis*. Scandinavian Institute of Business Analytics. ISBN 978-1512009309.

[6] "Choosing the Best Storage for Business Analytics". Dell.com. Retrieved 2012-06-25.

4.9 Further reading

- Bartlett, Randy (February 2013). *A Practitioner's Guide To Business Analytics: Using Data Analysis Tools to Improve Your Organization's Decision Making and Strategy*. McGraw-Hill. ISBN 978-0071807593.

- Saxena, Rahul; Anand Srinivasan (December 2012). *Business Analytics: A Practitioner's Guide (International Series in Operations Research & Management Science)*. Springer. ISBN 978-1461460794.

- Davenport, Thomas H.; Jeanne G. Harris (March 2007). *Competing on Analytics: The New Science of Winning*. Harvard Business School Press.

- McDonald, Mark; Tina Nunno (February 2007). *Creating Enterprise Leverage: The 2007 CIO Agenda*. Stamford, CT: Gartner, Inc.

- Stubbs, Evan (July 2011). *The Value of Business Analytics*. John Wiley & Sons.

- Ranadive, Vivek (2006-01-26). *The Power to Predict: How Real Time Businesses Anticipate Customer Needs, Create Opportunities, and Beat the Competition*. McGraw-Hill.

- Zabin, Jeffrey; Gresh Brebach (February 2004). *Precision Marketing*. John Wiley.

- Baker, Stephen (January 23, 2006). "Math Will Rock Your World". *BusinessWeek*. Retrieved 2007-09-19.

- Davenport, Thomas H. (January 1, 2006). "Competing on Analytics". *Harvard Business Review*.

- Pfeffer, Jeffrey; Robert I. Sutton (January 2006). "Evidence-Based Management". *Harvard Business Review*.

- Davenport, Thomas H.; Jeanne G. Harris (Summer 2005). "Automated Decision Making Comes of Age". *MIT Sloan Management Review*.

- Lewis, Michael (April 2004). *Moneyball: The Art of Winning an Unfair Game*. W.W. Norton & Co.

- Bonabeau, Eric (May 2003). "Don't Trust Your Gut". *Harvard Business Review*.

- Davenport, Thomas H.; Jeanne G. Harris; David W. De Long; Alvin L. Jacobson. "Data to Knowledge to Results: Building an Analytic Capability". *California Management Review* **43** (2): 117–138. doi:10.2307/41166078.

- Indian Bank Need Business Analysis Executives | Business Analytics Course

Chapter 5

Cross Industry Standard Process for Data Mining

Cross Industry Standard Process for Data Mining, commonly known by its acronym **CRISP-DM**,[1] was a data mining process model that describes commonly used approaches that data mining experts use to tackle problems. Polls conducted at one and the same website (KDNuggests) in 2002, 2004, 2007 and 2014 show that it was the leading methodology used by industry data miners who decided to respond to the survey.[2][3][4][5] The only other data mining standard named in these polls was SEMMA. However, 3-4 times as many people reported using CRISP-DM. A review and critique of data mining process models in 2009 called the CRISP-DM the "de facto standard for developing data mining and knowledge discovery projects."[6] Other reviews of CRISP-DM and data mining process models include Kurgan and Musilek's 2006 review,[7] and Azevedo and Santos' 2008 comparison of CRISP-DM and SEMMA.[8] Efforts to update the methodolgy started in 2006, but have As of 30 June 2015 not led to a new version, and the "Special Interest Group" (SIG) responsible along with the website has long disappeared (see History of CRISP-DM).

5.1 Major phases

CRISP-DM breaks the process of data mining into six major phases.[9]

The sequence of the phases is not strict and moving back and forth between different phases is always required. The arrows in the process diagram indicate the most important and frequent dependencies between phases. The outer circle in the diagram symbolizes the cyclic nature of data mining itself. A data mining process continues after a solution has been deployed. The lessons learned during the process can trigger new, often more focused business questions and subsequent data mining processes will benefit from the experiences of previous ones.

Business Understanding This initial phase focuses on understanding the project objectives and requirements from a business perspective, and then converting this knowledge into a data mining problem definition, and a preliminary plan designed to achieve the objectives. A decision model, especially one built using the Decision Model and Notation standard can be used.

Data Understanding The data understanding phase starts with an initial data collection and proceeds with activities in order to get familiar with the data, to identify data quality problems, to discover first insights into the data, or to detect interesting subsets to form hypotheses for hidden information.

Data Preparation The data preparation phase covers all activities to construct the final dataset (data that will be fed into the modeling tool(s)) from the initial raw data. Data preparation tasks are likely to be performed multiple times, and not in any prescribed order. Tasks include table, record, and attribute selection as well as transformation and cleaning of data for modeling tools.

Process diagram showing the relationship between the different phases of CRISP-DM

Modeling In this phase, various modeling techniques are selected and applied, and their parameters are calibrated to optimal values. Typically, there are several techniques for the same data mining problem type. Some techniques have specific requirements on the form of data. Therefore, stepping back to the data preparation phase is often needed.

Evaluation At this stage in the project you have built a model (or models) that appears to have high quality, from a data analysis perspective. Before proceeding to final deployment of the model, it is important to more thoroughly evaluate the model, and review the steps executed to construct the model, to be certain it properly achieves the business objectives. A key objective is to determine if there is some important business issue that has not been sufficiently considered. At the end of this phase, a decision on the use of the data mining results should be reached.

Deployment Creation of the model is generally not the end of the project. Even if the purpose of the model is to increase knowledge of the data, the knowledge gained will need to be organized and presented in a way that is useful to the customer. Depending on the requirements, the deployment phase can be as simple as generating a report or as complex as implementing a repeatable data scoring (e.g. segment allocation) or data mining process. In many cases it will be the customer, not the data analyst, who will carry out the deployment steps. Even if the analyst deploys the model it is important for the customer to understand up front the actions which will need to be carried out in order to actually make use of the created models.

5.2 History

CRISP-DM was conceived in 1996. In 1997 it got underway as a European Union project under the ESPRIT funding initiative. The project was led by five companies: SPSS, Teradata, Daimler AG, NCR Corporation and OHRA, an insurance company.

This core consortium brought different experiences to the project: ISL, later acquired and merged into SPSS Inc. The computer giant NCR Corporation produced the Teradata data warehouse and its own data mining software. Daimler-Benz had a significant data mining team. OHRA was just starting to explore the potential use of data mining.

The first version of the methodology was presented at the 4th CRISP-DM SIG Workshop in Brussels in March 1999,[10] and published as a step-by-step data mining guide later that year.[11]

Between 2006 and 2008 a CRISP-DM 2.0 SIG was formed and there were discussions about updating the CRISP-DM process model.[6][12] The current status of these efforts is not known. However, the original crisp-dm.org website cited in the reviews,[7][8] and the CRISP-DM 2.0 SIG website[6][12] are both no longer active.

While many non-IBM data mining practitioners use CRISP-DM,[2][3][4][6] IBM is the primary corporation that currently embraces the CRISP-DM process model. It makes some of the old CRISP-DM documents available for download[11] and it has incorporated it into its SPSS Modeler product.

5.3 References

[1] Shearer C., *The CRISP-DM model: the new blueprint for data mining*, J Data Warehousing (2000); 5:13—22.

[2] Gregory Piatetsky-Shapiro (2002); *KDnuggets Methodology Poll*

[3] Gregory Piatetsky-Shapiro (2004); *KDnuggets Methodology Poll*

[4] Gregory Piatetsky-Shapiro (2007); *KDnuggets Methodology Poll*

[5] Gregory Piatetsky-Shapiro (2014); *KDnuggets Methodology Poll*

[6] Óscar Marbán, Gonzalo Mariscal and Javier Segovia (2009); *A Data Mining & Knowledge Discovery Process Model*. In Data Mining and Knowledge Discovery in Real Life Applications, Book edited by: Julio Ponce and Adem Karahoca, ISBN 978-3-902613-53-0, pp. 438-453, February 2009, I-Tech, Vienna, Austria.

[7] Lukasz Kurgan and Petr Musilek (2006); *A survey of Knowledge Discovery and Data Mining process models*. The Knowledge Engineering Review. Volume 21 Issue 1, March 2006, pp 1 - 24, Cambridge University Press, New York, NY, USA doi: 10.1017/S0269888906000737.

[8] Azevedo, A. and Santos, M. F. (2008);KDD, SEMMA and CRISP-DM: a parallel overview. In Proceedings of the IADIS European Conference on Data Mining 2008, pp 182-185.

[9] Harper, Gavin; Stephen D. Pickett (August 2006). "Methods for mining HTS data". *Drug Discovery Today* **11** (15–16): 694–699. doi:10.1016/j.drudis.2006.06.006. PMID 16846796.

[10] Pete Chapman (1999); *The CRISP-DM User Guide.*

[11] Pete Chapman, Julian Clinton, Randy Kerber, Thomas Khabaza, Thomas Reinartz, Colin Shearer, and Rüdiger Wirth (2000); *CRISP-DM 1.0 Step-by-step data mining guides.*

[12] Colin Shearer (2006); *First CRISP-DM 2.0 Workshop Held*

Chapter 6

Customer analytics

Customer analytics is a process by which data from customer behavior is used to help make key business decisions via market segmentation and predictive analytics. This information is used by businesses for direct marketing, site selection, and customer relationship management. Marketing provides services in order to satisfy customers. With that in mind, the productive system is considered from its beginning at the production level, to the end of the cycle at the consumer. Customer analytics plays a very important role in the prediction of customer behavior today.[1]

6.1 Uses

Retail

Although until recently over 90% of retailers had limited visibility on their customers, with increasing investments in loyalty programs, customer tracking solutions and market research, this industry started increasing use of customer analytics in decisions ranging from product, promotion, price and distribution management.

Finance

Banks, insurance companies and pension funds make use of customer analytics in understanding customer lifetime value, identifying below-zero customers which are estimated to be around 30% of customer base, increasing cross-sales, managing customer attrition as well as migrating customers to lower cost channels in a targeted manner.

Community

Municipalities utilize customer analytics in an effort to lure retailers to their cities. Using psychographic variables, communities can be segmented based on attributes like personality, values, interests, and lifestyle. Using this information, communities can approach retailers that match their community's profile.

Customer relationship management

Analytical Customer Relationship Management, commonly abbreviated as CRM, enables measurement of and prediction from customer data to provide a 360° view of the client.

6.2 Predicting customer behavior

Forecasting buying habits and lifestyle preferences is a process of data mining and analysis. This information consists of many aspects like credit card purchases, magazine subscriptions, loyalty card membership, surveys, and voter registration.

Using these categories, profiles can be created for any organization's most profitable customers. When many of these potential customers are aggregated in a single area it indicates a fertile location for the business to situate. Using a drive time analysis, it is also possible to predict how far a given customer will drive to a particular location. Combining these sources of information, a dollar value can be placed on each household within a trade area detailing the likelihood that household will be worth to a company. Through customer analytics, companies can make decisions with confidence because every decision is based on facts and objective Data.

6.3   Data mining

There are two types of categories of data mining. Predictive models use previous customer interactions to predict future events while segmentation techniques are used to place customers with similar behaviors and attributes into distinct groups. This grouping can help marketers to optimize their campaign management and targeting processes.

6.4   See also

- Buyer decision processes
- Business analytics
- Data warehouse
- Psychographics
- Mattersight Corporation

6.5   References

[1] Kioumarsi et al., 2009

6.6   Further readling

- Kioumarsi, H., Khorshidi, K.J., Yahaya, Z.S., Van Cutsem, I., Zarafat, M., Rahman, W.A. (2009). Customer Satisfaction: The Case of Fresh Meat Eating Quality Preferences and the USDA Yield Grade Standard. Int'l Journal of Arts & Sciences (IJAS) Conference.

6.7   External links

- Wharton Customer Analytics Initiative
- http://www.babsonknowledge.org/analytics.pdf
- http://www.crmbuyer.com/story/49917.html

Chapter 7

Data Applied

Data Applied is a software vendor headquartered in Washington. Founded by a group of former Microsoft employees,[1] the company specializes in data mining, data visualization, and business intelligence environments.

7.1 Products

Data Applied implements a collection of visualization tools and algorithms for data analysis and data mining. The product supports several types of analytical tasks, including visual reporting, tree maps, time series forecasting, correlation analysis, outlier detection, decision trees, association rules, clustering, and self-organizing maps.

7.2 References

[1] New York Times: Ex-Microsofties Launch $500 'Meaning Machine' For Large Data Sets

7.3 External links

- Official Site

Chapter 8

Data mining in agriculture

Data mining in agriculture is a very recent research topic. It consists in the application of data mining techniques to agriculture. Recent technologies are nowadays able to provide a lot of information on agricultural-related activities, which can then be analyzed in order to find important information.[1] A related, but not equivalent term is precision agriculture.

8.1 Applications

8.1.1 Prediction of problematic wine fermentations

Wine is widely produced all around the world. The fermentation process of the wine is very important, because it can impact the productivity of wine-related industries and also the quality of wine. If we were able to predict how the fermentation is going to be at the early stages of the process, we could interfere with the process in order to guarantee a regular and smooth fermentation. Fermentations are nowadays studied by using different techniques, such as, for example, the k-means algorithm,[2] and a technique for classification based on the concept of biclustering.[3] Note that these works are different from the ones where a classification of different kinds of wine is performed. See the wiki page Classification of wine for more details.

8.1.2 Detection of diseases from sounds issued by animals

The detection of animal's diseases in farms can impact positively the productivity of the farm, because sick animals can cause contaminations. Moreover, the early detection of the diseases can allow the farmer to cure the animal as soon as the disease appears. Sounds issued by pigs can be analyzed for the detection of diseases. In particular, their coughs can be studied, because they indicate their sickness. A computational system is under development which is able to monitor pig sounds by microphones installed in the farm, and which is also able to discriminate among the different sounds that can be detected.[4]

8.1.3 Sorting apples by watercores

Before going to market, apples are checked and the ones showing some defects are removed. However, there are also invisible defects, that can spoil the apple flavor and look. An example of invisible defect is the watercore. This is an internal apple disorder that can affect the longevity of the fruit. Apples with slight or mild watercores are sweeter, but apples with moderate to sever degree of watercore cannot be stored for any length of time. Moreover, a few fruits with severe watercore could spoil a whole batch of apples. For this reason, a computational system is under study which takes X-ray photographs of the fruit while they run on conveyor belts, and which is also able to analyse (by data mining techniques) the taken pictures and estimate the probability that the fruit contains watercores.[5]

8.1.4   Optimizing pesticide use by data mining

Recent studies by agriculture researchers in Pakistan (one of the top four cotton producers of the world) showed that attempts of cotton crop yield maximization through pro-pesticide state policies have led to a dangerously high pesticide use. These studies have reported a negative correlation between pesticide use and crop yield in Pakistan. Hence excessive use (or abuse) of pesticides is harming the farmers with adverse financial, environmental and social impacts. By data mining the cotton Pest Scouting data along with the meteorological recordings it was shown that how pesticide use can be optimized (reduced). Clustering of data revealed interesting patterns of farmer practices along with pesticide use dynamics and hence help identify the reasons for this pesticide abuse.[6]

8.1.5   Explaining pesticide abuse by data mining

To monitor cotton growth, different government departments and agencies in Pakistan have been recording pest scouting, agriculture and metrological data for decades. Coarse estimates of just the cotton pest scouting data recorded stands at around 1.5 million records, and growing. The primary agro-met data recorded has never been digitized, integrated or standardized to give a complete picture, and hence cannot support decision making, thus requiring an Agriculture Data Warehouse. Creating a novel Pilot Agriculture Extension Data Warehouse followed by analysis through querying and data mining some interesting discoveries were made, such as pesticides sprayed at the wrong time, wrong pesticides used for the right reasons and temporal relationship between pesticide usage and day of the week.[7]

8.2   Literature

Since this research topic is quite recent, there is only one reference book. *Data Mining in Agriculture* is published by Springer and it is co-authored by Antonio Mucherino, Petraq Papajorgji and Panos Pardalos. A quick survey of the book can be found at this address. There are a few precision agriculture journals, such as Springer's Precision Agriculture or Elsevier's Computers and Electronics in Agriculture, but those are not exclusively devoted to data mining in agriculture.

8.3   Conferences

There are many conferences organized every year on data mining techniques and applications, but rather few of them consider problems arising in the agricultural field. To date, there is only one example of a conference completely devoted to applications in agriculture of data mining. It is organized by Georg Ruß. This is the conference web page.

8.4   References

[1] Mucherino, A.; Papajorgji, P.J.; Pardalos, P. (2009). *Data Mining in Agriculture, Springer*.

[2] Urtubia, A.; Perez-Correa, J.R.; Meurens, M.; Agosin, E. (2004). "Monitoring Large Scale Wine Fermentations with Infrared Spectroscopy". *Talanta 64(3)*: 778–784.

[3] Mucherino, A.; Urtubia, A. (2010). "Consistent Biclustering and Applications to Agriculture". *IbaI Conference Proceedings, Proceedings of the Industrial Conference on Data Mining (ICDM10), Workshop Data Mining in Agriculture (DMA10), Springer*: 105–113.

[4] Chedad, A.; Moshou, D.; Aerts, J.M.; Van Hirtum, A.; Ramon, H.; Berckmans, D. (2001). "Recognition System for Pig Cough based on Probabilistic Neural Networks". *Journal of Agricultural Engineering Research 79(4)*: 449–457.

[5] Schatzki, T.F.; Haff, R.P.; Young, R.; Can, I.; Le, L-C.; Toyofuku, N. (1997). "Defect Detection in Apples by Means of X-ray Imaging". *Transactions of the American Society of Agricultural Engineers 40(5)*: 1407–1415.

[6] Abdullah, Ahsan; Brobst, Stephen; Pervaiz, Ijaz; Umar, Muhammad; Nisar, Azhar (2004). *Learning Dynamics of Pesticide Abuse through Data Mining* (PDF). Australasian Workshop on Data Mining and Web Intelligence, Dunedin, New Zealand.

[7] Abdullah, Ahsan; Hussain, Amir (2006). "Data Mining a New Pilot Agriculture Extension Data Warehouse" (PDF). *Journal of Research and Practice in Information Technology, Vol. 38, No. 3, August 2006*: 229–249.

Chapter 9

Data mining in meteorology

For other uses of the root word "meteor", see Meteor (disambiguation). For about data mining, see Data mining.

Meteorology is the interdisciplinary scientific study of the atmosphere. It observes the changes in temperature, air pressure, moisture and wind direction. Usually, temperature, pressure, wind measurements and humidity are the variables that are measured by a thermometer, barometer, anemometer, and hygrometer, respectively. There are many methods of collecting data and Radar, Lidar, satellites are some of them. Weather forecasts are made by collecting quantitative data about the current state of the atmosphere. The main issue arise in this prediction is, it involves high-dimensional characters. To overcome this issue, it is necessary to first analyze and simplify the data before proceeding with other analysis. Some data mining techniques are appropriate in this context.

9.1   What is Data mining?

Data mining, the extraction of hidden predictive information from large databases, is a powerful new technology with great potential to analyze important information in data warehouses. Consequently, data mining consists of more than collecting and analyzing data, it also includes analyze and predictions. The tools which are used for analysis can include statistical models, mathematical algorithms and machine learning methods. These methods include algorithms that improve their performance automatically through experience, such as neural networks or decision trees[1]

The network architecture and signal process used to model nervous systems can roughly be divided into three categories, each based on a different philosophy.

1. Feedforward neural network: the input information defines the initial signals into set of output signals.[2]

2. Feedback network: the input information defines the initial activity state of a feedback system, and after state transitions, the asymptotic final state is identified as the outcome of the computation.[3]

3. Neighboring cells in a neural network compete in their activities by means of mutual lateral interactions, and develop adaptively into specific detectors of different signal patterns. In this category, learning is called competitive, unsupervised learning or self-organizing.[4]

9.1.1   Self-organizing Maps

Self-Organizing Map (SOM) is one of the most popular neural network models, which is especially suitable for high dimensional data visualization, clustering and modeling. It uses an unsupervised learning for creating a set of prototype vectors representing the data. The SOM was introduced to meteorological and climatic sciences in late 1990s as a clustering and pattern recognition method.[5] Nowadays, Self-Organized maps have been applied in several meteorological problems, such as classifying climate modes, cloud classification,[6] classification of TEMP data,[7] extreme weather and rainfall pattern analysis. The Self-Organizing Map projects high-dimensional input data onto a low dimensional (usually two-dimensional) space.[8] Because it preserves the neighborhood relations of the input data, the SOM is a topology-preserving technique. There are many types of topologies used in SOM: grid, hexagonal, random are some of them.[9] The output neurons are arranged according to the given topology. The distances between neurons are calculated using a distance function.[10] There are several distance functions which can be used such as Euclidean distance, box distance, link distance and Manhattan distance.

According to the first input of the input vector, System chooses the output neuron (winning neuron) that closely matches with the given input vector. Then determining a neighborhood of excited neurons around the winner; and finally, updating all of the excited neurons. It must select the neighborhood function that permits to calculate the nodes "nearest" to the winner.[11] Some neighborhood functions are the Gaussian, the Bubble and the EP.[12] The outcome weight vectors of the SOM nodes are reshaped back to have characteristic data patterns. This learning procedure leads to a topologically ordered mapping of the input data. Similar patterns are mapped onto neighboring regions on the map, while dissimilar patterns are located further apart.

9.2   References

[1] Seifert, W. (2004). "Data Mining:An Overview". *CRS*.

[2] Kohonen, T. (2002). "The Self-Organizing Map.". *IEEE*. pp. 1464–1480.

[3] Kohonen, T. (2002). "The Self-Organizing Map.". *IEEE*. pp. 1464–1480.

[4] Liu, Y., & Weisberg, R. H. "A Review of Self-Organizing Map Applications in Meteorology and Oceanography". *Self Organizing Maps - Applications and Novel Algorithm Design* . p. 2011.

[5] COFIÑO, A., GUTIÉRREZ, J., JAKUBIAK, B., & MELONEK, M. (2003). "IMPLEMENTATION OF DATA MINING TECHNIQUES FOR METEOROLOGICAL APPLICATIONS". *World Scientific*. pp. 215–240.

[6] Hong Y., HSU, K., SOROOSHIAN, S., & GAO, X. . (2004). "Precipitation Estimation from Remotely Sensed Imagery Using an Artificial Neural.". *JOURNAL OF APPLIED METEOROLOGY* **43**. pp. 1834–1852.

[7] Lahoz, D., & Miguel, M. S. (2004). "CLASSIFICATION TEMP DATA WITH SELF-ORGANIZING MAPS.". *Monografías del Seminario Matemático García de Galdeano*. pp. 389–397.

[8] Liu, Y., & Weisberg, R. H. "A Review of Self-Organizing Map Applications in Meteorology and Oceanography". *Self Organizing Maps - Applications and Novel Algorithm Design* . p. 2011.

[9] Lahoz, D., & Miguel, M. S. (2004). "CLASSIFICATION TEMP DATA WITH SELF-ORGANIZING MAPS.". *Monografías del Seminario Matemático García de Galdeano*. pp. 389–397.

[10] Lahoz, D., & Miguel, M. S. (2004). "CLASSIFICATION TEMP DATA WITH SELF-ORGANIZING MAPS.". *Monografías del Seminario Matemático García de Galdeano*. pp. 389–397.

[11] Lahoz, D., & Miguel, M. S. (2004). "CLASSIFICATION TEMP DATA WITH SELF-ORGANIZING MAPS.". *Monografías del Seminario Matemático García de Galdeano*. pp. 389–397.

[12] Lahoz, D., & Miguel, M. S. (2004). "CLASSIFICATION TEMP DATA WITH SELF-ORGANIZING MAPS.". *Monografías del Seminario Matemático García de Galdeano*. pp. 389–397.

9.3   External links

- Data Mining to Classify Fog Events by Applying Cost-Sensitive Classifier

Chapter 10

Educational data mining

Educational Data Mining (EDM) describes a research field concerned with the application of data mining, machine learning and statistics to information generated from educational settings (e.g., universities and intelligent tutoring systems). At a high level, the field seeks to develop and improve methods for exploring this data, which often has multiple levels of meaningful hierarchy, in order to discover new insights about how people learn in the context of such settings.[1] In doing so, EDM has contributed to theories of learning investigated by researchers in educational psychology and the learning sciences.[2] The field is closely tied to that of learning analytics, and the two have been compared and contrasted.[3]

10.1 Definition

Educational Data Mining refers to techniques, tools, and research designed for automatically extracting meaning from large repositories of data generated by or related to people's learning activities in educational settings. Quite often, this data is extensive, fine-grained, and precise. For example, several learning management systems (LMSs) track information such as when each student accessed each learning object, how many times they accessed it, and how many minutes the learning object was displayed on the user's computer screen. As another example, Intelligent tutoring systems record data every time a learner submits a solution to a problem; they may collect the time of the submission, whether or not the solution matches the expected solution, the amount of time that has passed since the last submission, the order in which solution components were entered into the interface, etc. The precision of this data is such that even a fairly short session with a computer-based learning environment (*e.g.*, 30 minutes) may produce a large amount of process data for analysis.

In other cases, the data is less fine-grained. For example, a student's university transcript may contain a temporally ordered list of courses taken by the student, the grade that the student earned in each course, and when the student selected or changed his or her academic major. EDM leverages both types of data to discover meaningful information about different types of learners and how they learn, the structure of domain knowledge, and the effect of instructional strategies embedded within various learning environments. These analyses provide new information that would be difficult to discern by looking at the raw data. For example, analyzing data from an LMS may reveal a relationship between the learning objects that a student accessed during the course and their final course grade. Similarly, analyzing student transcript data may reveal a relationship between a student's grade in a particular course and their decision to change their academic major. Such information provides insight into the design of learning environments, which allows students, teachers, school administrators, and educational policy makers to make informed decisions about how to interact with, provide, and manage educational resources.

10.2 History

While the analysis of educational data is not itself a new practice, recent advances in educational technology, including the increase in computing power and the ability to log fine-grained data about students' use of a computer-based learning environment, have led to an increased interest in developing techniques for analyzing the large amounts of data generated in educational settings. This interest translated into a series of EDM workshops held from 2000-2007 as part of several international research conferences.[4] In 2008, a group of researchers established what has become an annual international research conference on EDM, the first of which took place in Montreal, Canada.[5]

As interest in EDM continued to increase, EDM researchers established an academic journal in 2009, the Journal of Educational Data Mining, for sharing and disseminating research results. In 2011, EDM researchers established the International Educational Data Mining Society to connect EDM researchers and continue to grow the field.

With the introduction of public educational data repositories in 2008, such as the Pittsburgh Science of Learning Centre's (PSLC) DataShop and the National Center for Education Statistics (NCES), public data sets have made educational data mining more accessible and feasible, contributing to its growth.[6]

10.3   Goals

Baker and Yacef [7] identified the following four goals of EDM:

1. **Predicting students' future learning behavior** – With the use of student modeling, this goal can be achieved by creating student models that incorporate the learner's characteristics, including detailed information such as their knowledge, behaviours and motivation to learn. The user experience of the learner and their overall satisfaction with learning are also measured.

2. **Discovering or improving domain models** – Through the various methods and applications of EDM, discovery of new and improvements to existing models is possible. Examples include illustrating the educational content to engage learners and determining optimal instructional sequences to support the student's learning style.

3. **Studying the effects of educational support** that can be achieved through learning systems.

4. **Advancing scientific knowledge about learning and learners** by building and incorporating student models, the field of EDM research and the technology and software used.

10.4   Users and Stakeholders

There are four main users and stakeholders involved with educational data mining. These include:

- **Learners** - Learners are interested in understanding student needs and methods to improve the learner's experience and performance.[8] For example, learners can also benefit from the discovered knowledge by using the EDM tools to suggest activities and resources that they can use based on their interactions with the online learning tool and insights from past or similar learners.[9] For younger learners, educational data mining can also inform parents about their child's learning progress.[10] It is also necessary to effectively group learners in an online environment. The challenge is to learn these groups based on the complex data as well as develop actionable models to interpret these groups.[11]

- **Educators** - Educators attempt to understand the learning process and the methods they can use to improve their teaching methods.[8] Educators can use the applications of EDM to determine how to organize and structure the curriculum, the best methods to deliver course information and the tools to use to engage their learners for optimal learning outcomes.[12] In particular, the distillation of data for human judgment technique provides an opportunity for educators to benefit from EDM because it enables educators to quickly identify behavioural patterns, which can support their teaching methods during the duration of the course or to improve future courses. Educators can determine indicators that show student satisfaction and engagement of course material, and also monitor learning progress.[12]

- **Researchers** - Researchers focus on the development and the evaluation of data mining techniques for effectiveness.[8] A yearly international conference for researchers began in 2008, followed by the establishment of the Journal of Educational Data Mining in 2009. The wide range of topics in EDM ranges from using data mining to improve institutional effectiveness to student performance.[13]

- **Administrators** - Administrators are responsible for allocating the resources for implementation in institutions.[8] As institutions are increasingly held responsible for student success, the administering of EDM applications are becoming more common in educational settings.[13] Faculty and advisors are becoming more proactive in identifying and addressing at-risk students.[13] However, it is sometimes a challenge to get the information to the decision makers to administer the application in a timely and efficient manner.[13]

10.5   Phases of Educational Data Mining

As research in the field of educational data mining has continued to grow, a myriad of data mining techniques have been applied to a variety of educational contexts. In each case, the goal is to translate raw data into meaningful information about the learning process in order to make better decisions about the design and trajectory of a learning environment. Thus, EDM generally consists of four phases:[2][4]

1. The first phase of the EDM process (not counting pre-processing) is discovering relationships in data. This involves searching through a repository of data from an educational environment with the goal of finding consistent relationships between variables. Several algorithms for identifying such relationships have been utilized, including classification, regression, clustering, factor analysis, social network analysis, association rule mining, and sequential pattern mining.

2. Discovered relationships must then be validated in order to avoid overfitting.

3. Validated relationships are applied to make predictions about future events in the learning environment.

4. Predictions are used to support decision-making processes and policy decisions.

During phases 3 and 4, data is often visualized or in some other way distilled for human judgment.[2] A large amount of research has been conducted in best practices for visualizing data.

10.6   Main Approaches

Of the general categories of methods mentioned, prediction, clustering and relationship mining are considered universal methods across all types of data mining; however, **Discovery with Models** and **Distillation of Data for Human Judgment** are considered more prominent approaches within educational data mining.[6]

10.6.1   Discovery with Models

In the Discovery with Model method, a model is developed via prediction, clustering or by human reasoning knowledge engineering and then used as a component in another analysis, namely in prediction and relationship mining.[6] In the **prediction** method use, the created model's predictions are used to predict a new variable.[6] For the use of **relationship mining**, the created model enables the analysis between new predictions and additional variables in the study.[6] In many cases, discovery with models uses validated prediction models that have proven generalizability across contexts.

Key applications of this method include discovering relationships between student behaviors, characteristics and contextual variables in the learning environment.[6] Further discovery of broad and specific research questions across a wide range of contexts can also be explored using this method.

10.6.2   Distillation of Data for Human Judgment

Humans can make inferences about data that may be beyond the scope in which an automated data mining method provides.[6] For the use of education data mining, data is distilled for human judgment for two key purposes, identification and classification.[6]

For the purpose of identification, data is distilled to enable humans to identify well-known patterns, which may otherwise be difficult to interpret. For example, the learning curve, classic to educational studies, is a pattern that clearly reflects the relationship between learning and experience over time.

Data is also distilled for the purposes of classifying features of data, which for educational data mining, is used to support the development of the prediction model. Classification helps expedite the development of the prediction model, tremendously.

The goal of this method is to summarize and present the information in a useful, interactive and visually appealing way in order to understand the large amounts of education data and to support decision making.[8] In particular, this method is beneficial to educators in understanding usage information and effectiveness in course activities.[8] Key applications for the distillation of data for human judgment include identifying patterns in student learning, behavior, opportunities for collaboration and labeling data for future uses in prediction models.[6]

10.7   Applications

A list of the primary applications of EDM is provided by Cristobal Romero and Sebastian Ventura.[4] In their taxonomy, the areas of EDM application are:

- Analysis and visualization of data

- Providing feedback for supporting instructors

- Recommendations for students

- Predicting student performance

- Student modeling

- Detecting undesirable student behaviors

- Grouping students

- Social network analysis

- Developing concept maps

- Constructing courseware - EDM can be applied to course management systems such as open source Moodle. Moodle contains usage data that includes various activities by users such as test results, amount of readings completed and participation in discussion forums.[13] Data mining tools can be used to customize learning activities for each user and adapt the pace in which the student completes the course. This is in particularly beneficial for online courses with varying levels of competency.[13]

- Planning and scheduling

New research on mobile learning environments also suggests that data mining can be useful. Data mining can be used to help provide personalized content to mobile users, despite the differences in managing content between mobile devices and standard PCs and web browsers.[13]

New EDM applications will focus on allowing non-technical users use and engage in data mining tools and activities, making data collection and processing more accessible for all users of EDM.[13] Examples include statistical and visualization tools that analyzes social networks and their influence on learning outcomes and productivity.[14]

10.8 Courses

In October 2013, Coursera offered a free online course on "Big Data in Education" that teaches how and when to use key methods for EDM.[15] This course moved to edX in the summer of 2015.[16] A course archive is now available online.[17]

Teachers College, Columbia University offers a MS in Learning Analytics.[18]

10.9 Publication Venues

Considerable amounts of EDM work are published at the peer-reviewed International Conference on Educational Data Mining, organized by the International Educational Data Mining Society.

- 1st International Conference on Educational Data Mining (2008) -- Montreal, Canada

- 2nd International Conference on Educational Data Mining (2009) -- Cordoba, Spain

- 3rd International Conference on Educational Data Mining (2010) -- Pittsburgh, USA

- 4th International Conference on Educational Data Mining (2011) -- Eindhoven, Netherlands

- 5th International Conference on Educational Data Mining (2012) -- Chania, Greece

- 6th International Conference on Educational Data Mining (2013) -- Memphis, USA

- 7th International Conference on Educational Data Mining (2014) -- London, UK

- 8th International Conference on Educational Data Mining (2015) -- Madrid, Spain

EDM papers are also published in the Journal of Educational Data Mining (JEDM).

Many EDM papers are routinely published in related conferences, such as Artificial Intelligence and Education, Intelligent Tutoring Systems, and User Modeling and Adaptive Personalization.

In 2011, Chapman & Hall/CRC Press, Taylor and Francis Group published the first Handbook of Educational Data Mining. This resource was created for those that are interested in participating in the educational data mining community.[14]

10.10 Contests

In 2010, the Association for Computing Machinery's KDD Cup was conducted using data from an educational setting. The data set was provided by the Pittsburgh Science of Learning Center's DataShop, and it consisted of over 1,000,000 data points from students using a Cognitive Tutor. Six hundred teams competed for over 8,000 USD in prize money (which was donated by Facebook). The goal for contestants was to design an algorithm that, after learning from the provided data, would make the most accurate predictions from new data. The winners submitted an algorithm that utilized feature generation (a form of representation learning), random forests, and Bayesian networks.

10.11 Costs and Challenges

Along with technological advancements are costs and challenges associated with implementing EDM applications. These include the costs to store logged data and the cost associated with hiring staff dedicated to managing data systems.[19] Moreover, data systems may not always integrate seamlessly with one another and even with the support of statistical and visualization tools, creating one simplified version of the data can be difficult.[19] Furthermore, choosing which data to mine and analyze can also be challenging,[19] making the initial stages very time consuming and labor-intensive. From beginning to end, the EDM strategy and implementation requires one to uphold privacy and ethics[19] for all stakeholders involved.

10.12   Criticisms

- **Generalizability** - Research in EDM may be specific to the particular educational setting and time in which the research was conducted, and as such, may not be generalizable to other institutions. Research also indicates that the field of educational data mining is concentrated in North America and western cultures and subsequently, other countries and cultures may not be represented in the research and findings.[7] Development of future models should consider applications across multiple contexts.[13]

- **Privacy** - Individual privacy is a continued concern for the application of data mining tools. With free, accessible and user-friendly tools in the market, students and their families may be at risk from the information that learners provide to the learning system, in hopes to receive feedback that will benefit their future performance. As users become savvy in their understanding of online privacy, administrators of educational data mining tools need to be proactive in protecting the privacy of their users and be transparent about how and with whom the information will be used and shared. Development of EDM tools should consider protecting individual privacy while still advancing the research in this field.

- **Plagiarism** - Plagiarism detection is an ongoing challenge for educators and faculty whether in the classroom or online. However, due to the complexities associated with detecting and preventing digital plagiarism in particular, educational data mining tools are not currently sophisticated enough to accurately address this issue. Thus, the development of predictive capability in plagiarism-related issues should be an area of focus in future research.

- **Adoption** - It is unknown how widespread the adoption of EDM is and the extent to which institutions have applied and considered implementing an EDM strategy.[13] As such, it is unclear whether there are any barriers that prevent users from adopting EDM in their educational settings.

10.13   See also

- Learning analytics

- Data mining

- Machine learning

- Statistics

- Education

- Big data

- Educational technology

- Glossary of education terms

10.14   References

[1] "EducationalDataMining.org". 2013. Retrieved 2013-07-15.

[2] R. Baker (2010) Data Mining for Education. In McGaw, B., Peterson, P., Baker, E. (Eds.) International Encyclopedia of Education (3rd edition), vol. 7, pp. 112-118. Oxford, UK: Elsevier.

[3] G. Siemens, R.S.j.d. Baker (2012). "Learning analytics and educational data mining: towards communication and collaboration". *Proceedings of the 2nd International Conference on Learning Analytics and Knowledge*: 252–254.

[4] C. Romero, S. Ventura. Educational Data Mining: A Review of the State-of-the-Art. IEEE Transaction on Systems, Man, and Cybernetics, Part C: Applications and Reviews. 40(**6**), 601-618, 2010.

[5] "http://educationaldatamining.org/EDM2008/" Retrieved 2013-09-04

[6] Baker, Ryan. "Data Mining for Education" (PDF). oxford, UK: Elsevier. Retrieved 9 February 2014.

[7] Baker, R.S.; Yacef, K (2009). "The state of educational data mining in 2009: A review and future visions". *JEDM-Journal of Educational Data Mining* **1** (1): 2017.

[8] Romero, Cristobal; Ventura, Sebastian (JAN-FEB 2013). "WIREs Data Mining Knowl Discov". *Wiley Interdisciplinary Reviews: Data Mining and Knowledge Discovery* **3** (1): 12–27. doi:10.1002/widm.1075. Check date values in: |date= (help);

[9] Romero, Cristobal; Ventura, Sebastian (2007). "Educational data mining: A survey from 1995 to 2005". *Expert Systems with Applications* **33** (1): 135–146.

[10] "Assessing the Economic Impact of Copyright Reform in the Area of Technology-Enhanced Learning". Retrieved 6 April 2014. |first1= missing |last1= in Authors list (help)

[11] Azarnoush, Bahareh, et al. "Toward a Framework for Learner Segmentation." JEDM-Journal of Educational Data Mining 5.2 (2013): 102-126.

[12] U.S. Department of Education, Office of Educational Technology. "Enhancing Teaching and Learning Through Educational Data Mining and Learning Analytics: An Issue Brief" (PDF). Retrieved 30 March 2014.

[13] Huebner, Richard A. "A survey of educational data-mining research" (PDF). Research in Higher Education Journal. Retrieved 30 March 2014.

[14] *Handbook of educational data mining.* CRC Press. 2010. |first1= missing |last1= in Authors list (help)

[15] "Big Data in Education". Retrieved 30 March 2014. |first1= missing |last1= in Authors list (help)

[16] "Big Data in Education". Retrieved 13 October 2015. |first1= missing |last1= in Authors list (help)

[17] "Big Data in Education". Retrieved 11 April 2014.

[18] "Learning Analytics | Teachers College Columbia University". *www.tc.columbia.edu.* Retrieved 2015-10-13.

[19] "How Can Educational Data Mining and Learning Analytics Improve and Personalize Education?". Retrieved 9 April 2014. |first1= missing |last1= in Authors list (help)

Chapter 11

Examples of data mining

See also: Category:Applied data mining.

Data mining has been used in many applications. Some notable examples of usage are:

11.1 Games

Since the early 1960s, with the availability of oracles for certain combinatorial games, also called tablebases (e.g. for 3x3-chess) with any beginning configuration, small-board dots-and-boxes, small-board-hex, and certain endgames in chess, dots-and-boxes, and hex; a new area for data mining has been opened. This is the extraction of human-usable strategies from these oracles. Current pattern recognition approaches do not seem to fully acquire the high level of abstraction required to be applied successfully. Instead, extensive experimentation with the tablebases – combined with an intensive study of tablebase-answers to well designed problems, and with knowledge of prior art (i.e., pre-tablebase knowledge) – is used to yield insightful patterns. Berlekamp (in dots-and-boxes, etc.) and John Nunn (in chess endgames) are notable examples of researchers doing this work, though they were not – and are not – involved in tablebase generation.

11.2 Business

In business, data mining is the analysis of historical business activities, stored as static data in data warehouse databases. The goal is to reveal hidden patterns and trends. Data mining software uses advanced pattern recognition algorithms to sift through large amounts of data to assist in discovering previously unknown strategic business information. Examples of what businesses use data mining for include performing market analysis to identify new product bundles, finding the root cause of manufacturing problems, to prevent customer attrition and acquire new customers, cross-selling to existing customers, and profiling customers with more accuracy.[1]

- In today's world raw data is being collected by companies at an exploding rate. For example, Walmart processes over 20 million point-of-sale transactions every day. This information is stored in a centralized database, but would be useless without some type of data mining software to analyze it. If Walmart analyzed their point-of-sale data with data mining techniques they would be able to determine sales trends, develop marketing campaigns, and more accurately predict customer loyalty.[2][3]

- Categorization of the items available in the e-commerce site is a fundamental problem. A correct item categorization system is essential for user experience as it helps determine the items relevant to him for search and browsing. Item categorization can be formulated as a supervised classification problem in data mining where the categories are the target classes and the features are the words composing some textual description of the items. One of the approaches is to find groups initially which are similar and place them together in a latent group. Now given a new item, first classify into a latent group which is called coarse level classification. Then, do a second round of classification to find the category to which the item belongs to.[4]

- Every time a credit card or a store loyalty card is being used, or a warranty card is being filled, data is being collected about the users behavior. Many people find the amount of information stored about us from companies, such as Google, Facebook, and Amazon, disturbing and are concerned about privacy. Although there is the potential for our personal data to be used in harmful, or unwanted, ways it is also being used to make our lives better. For example, Ford and Audi hope to one day collect information about customer driving patterns so they can recommend safer routes and warn drivers about dangerous road conditions.[5]

- Data mining in customer relationship management applications can contribute significantly to the bottom line. Rather than randomly contacting a prospect or customer through a call center or sending mail, a company can concentrate its efforts on prospects that are predicted to have a high likelihood of responding to an offer. More sophisticated methods may be used to optimize resources across campaigns so that one may predict to which channel and to which offer an individual is most likely to respond (across all potential offers). Additionally, sophisticated applications could be used to automate mailing. Once the results from data mining (potential prospect/customer and channel/offer) are determined, this "sophisticated application" can either automatically send an e-mail or a regular mail. Finally, in cases where many people will take an action without an offer, "uplift modeling" can be used to determine which people have the greatest increase in response if given an offer. Uplift modeling thereby enables marketers to focus mailings and offers on persuadable people, and not to send offers to people who will buy the product without an offer. Data clustering can also be used to automatically discover the segments or groups within a customer data set.

- Businesses employing data mining may see a return on investment, but also they recognize that the number of predictive models can quickly become very large. For example, rather than using one model to predict how many customers will churn, a business may choose to build a separate model for each region and customer type. In situations where a large number of models need to be maintained, some businesses turn to more automated data mining methodologies.

- Data mining can be helpful to human resources (HR) departments in identifying the characteristics of their most successful employees. Information obtained – such as universities attended by highly successful employees – can help HR focus recruiting efforts accordingly. Additionally, Strategic Enterprise Management applications help a company translate corporate-level goals, such as profit and margin share targets, into operational decisions, such as production plans and workforce levels.[6]

- Market basket analysis, relates to data-mining use in retail sales. If a clothing store records the purchases of customers, a data mining system could identify those customers who favor silk shirts over cotton ones. Although some explanations of relationships may be difficult, taking advantage of it is easier. The example deals with association rules within transaction-based data. Not all data are transaction based and logical, or inexact rules may also be present within a database.

- Market basket analysis has been used to identify the purchase patterns of the Alpha Consumer. Analyzing the data collected on this type of user has allowed companies to predict future buying trends and forecast supply demands.

- Data mining is a highly effective tool in the catalog marketing industry. Catalogers have a rich database of history of their customer transactions for millions of customers dating back a number of years. Data mining tools can identify patterns among customers and help identify the most likely customers to respond to upcoming mailing campaigns.

- Data mining for business applications can be integrated into a complex modeling and decision making process.[7] Reactive business intelligence (RBI) advocates a "holistic" approach that integrates data mining, modeling, and interactive visualization into an end-to-end discovery and continuous innovation process powered by human and automated learning.[8]

- In the area of decision making, the RBI approach has been used to mine knowledge that is progressively acquired from the decision maker, and then self-tune the decision method accordingly.[9] The relation between the quality of a data mining system and the amount of investment that the decision maker is willing to make was formalized by providing an economic perspective on the value of "extracted knowledge" in terms of its payoff to the organization[7]

This decision-theoretic classification framework[7] was applied to a real-world semiconductor wafer manufacturing line, where decision rules for effectively monitoring and controlling the semiconductor wafer fabrication line were developed.[10]

- An example of data mining related to an integrated-circuit (IC) production line is described in the paper "Mining IC Test Data to Optimize VLSI Testing."[11] In this paper, the application of data mining and decision analysis to the problem of die-level functional testing is described. Experiments mentioned demonstrate the ability to apply a system of mining historical die-test data to create a probabilistic model of patterns of die failure. These patterns are then utilized to decide, in real time, which die to test next and when to stop testing. This system has been shown, based on experiments with historical test data, to have the potential to improve profits on mature IC products. Other examples[12][13] of the application of data mining methodologies in semiconductor manufacturing environments suggest that data mining methodologies may be particularly useful when data is scarce, and the various physical and chemical parameters that affect the process exhibit highly complex interactions. Another implication is that on-line monitoring of the semiconductor manufacturing process using data mining may be highly effective.

11.3   Science and engineering

In recent years, data mining has been used widely in the areas of science and engineering, such as bioinformatics, genetics, medicine, education and electrical power engineering.

- In the study of human genetics, sequence mining helps address the important goal of understanding the mapping relationship between the inter-individual variations in human DNA sequence and the variability in disease susceptibility. In simple terms, it aims to find out how the changes in an individual's DNA sequence affects the risks of developing common diseases such as cancer, which is of great importance to improving methods of diagnosing, preventing, and treating these diseases. One data mining method that is used to perform this task is known as multifactor dimensionality reduction.[14]

- In the area of electrical power engineering, data mining methods have been widely used for condition monitoring of high voltage electrical equipment. The purpose of condition monitoring is to obtain valuable information on, for example, the status of the insulation (or other important safety-related parameters). Data clustering techniques – such as the self-organizing map (SOM), have been applied to vibration monitoring and analysis of transformer on-load tap-changers (OLTCS). Using vibration monitoring, it can be observed that each tap change operation generates a signal that contains information about the condition of the tap changer contacts and the drive mechanisms. Obviously, different tap positions will generate different signals. However, there was considerable variability amongst normal condition signals for exactly the same tap position. SOM has been applied to detect abnormal conditions and to hypothesize about the nature of the abnormalities.[15]

- Data mining methods have been applied to dissolved gas analysis (DGA) in power transformers. DGA, as a diagnostics for power transformers, has been available for many years. Methods such as SOM has been applied to analyze generated data and to determine trends which are not obvious to the standard DGA ratio methods (such as Duval Triangle).[15]

- In educational research, where data mining has been used to study the factors leading students to choose to engage in behaviors which reduce their learning,[16] and to understand factors influencing university student retention.[17] A similar example of social application of data mining is its use in expertise finding systems, whereby descriptors of human expertise are extracted, normalized, and classified so as to facilitate the finding of experts, particularly in scientific and technical fields. In this way, data mining can facilitate institutional memory.

- Data mining methods of biomedical data facilitated by domain ontologies,[18] mining clinical trial data,[19] and traffic analysis using SOM.[20]

- In adverse drug reaction surveillance, the Uppsala Monitoring Centre has, since 1998, used data mining methods to routinely screen for reporting patterns indicative of emerging drug safety issues in the WHO global database of 4.6 million suspected adverse drug reaction incidents.[21] Recently, similar methodology has been developed to mine large collections of electronic health records for temporal patterns associating drug prescriptions to medical diagnoses.[22]

- Data mining has been applied to software artifacts within the realm of software engineering: Mining Software Repositories.

11.4 Human rights

Data mining of government records – particularly records of the justice system (i.e., courts, prisons) – enables the discovery of systemic human rights violations in connection to generation and publication of invalid or fraudulent legal records by various government agencies.[23][24]

11.5 Medical data mining

Some machine learning algorithms can be applied in medical field as second-opinion diagnostic tools and as tools for the knowledge extraction phase in the process of knowledge discovery in databases. One of these classifiers (called *Prototype exemplar learning classifier* (PEL-C)[25] is able to discover syndromes as well as atypical clinical cases.

In 2011, the case of Sorrell v. IMS Health, Inc., decided by the Supreme Court of the United States, ruled that pharmacies may share information with outside companies. This practice was authorized under the 1st Amendment of the Constitution, protecting the "freedom of speech."[26] However, the passage of the Health Information Technology for Economic and Clinical Health Act (HITECH Act) helped to initiate the adoption of the electronic health record (EHR) and supporting technology in the United States.[27] The HITECH Act was signed into law on February 17, 2009 as part of the American Recovery and Reinvestment Act (ARRA) and helped to open the door to medical data mining.[28] Prior to the signing of this law, estimates of only 20% of United States-based physicians were utilizing electronic patient records.[27] Søren Brunak notes that "the patient record becomes as information-rich as possible" and thereby "maximizes the data mining opportunities."[27] Hence, electronic patient records further expands the possibilities regarding medical data mining thereby opening the door to a vast source of medical data analysis.

11.6 Spatial data mining

Spatial data mining is the application of data mining methods to spatial data. The end objective of spatial data mining is to find patterns in data with respect to geography. So far, data mining and Geographic Information Systems (GIS) have existed as two separate technologies, each with its own methods, traditions, and approaches to visualization and data analysis. Particularly, most contemporary GIS have only very basic spatial analysis functionality. The immense explosion in geographically referenced data occasioned by developments in IT, digital mapping, remote sensing, and the global diffusion of GIS emphasizes the importance of developing data-driven inductive approaches to geographical analysis and modeling.

Data mining offers great potential benefits for GIS-based applied decision-making. Recently, the task of integrating these two technologies has become of critical importance, especially as various public and private sector organizations possessing huge databases with thematic and geographically referenced data begin to realize the huge potential of the information contained therein. Among those organizations are:

- offices requiring analysis or dissemination of geo-referenced statistical data

- public health services searching for explanations of disease clustering

- environmental agencies assessing the impact of changing land-use patterns on climate change

- geo-marketing companies doing customer segmentation based on spatial location.

Challenges in Spatial mining: Geospatial data repositories tend to be very large. Moreover, existing GIS datasets are often splintered into feature and attribute components that are conventionally archived in hybrid data management systems. Algorithmic requirements differ substantially for relational (attribute) data management and for topological (feature) data management.[29] Related to this is the range and diversity of geographic data formats, which present unique challenges. The digital geographic data revolution is creating new types of data formats beyond the traditional "vector" and "raster" formats. Geographic data repositories increasingly include ill-structured data, such as imagery and geo-referenced multimedia.[30]

There are several critical research challenges in geographic knowledge discovery and data mining. Miller and Han[31] offer the following list of emerging research topics in the field:

- **Developing and supporting geographic data warehouses (GDW's)**: Spatial properties are often reduced to simple aspatial attributes in mainstream data warehouses. Creating an integrated GDW requires solving issues of spatial and temporal data interoperability – including differences in semantics, referencing systems, geometry, accuracy, and position.

- **Better spatio-temporal representations in geographic knowledge discovery**: Current geographic knowledge discovery (GKD) methods generally use very simple representations of geographic objects and spatial relationships. Geographic data mining methods should recognize more complex geographic objects (i.e., lines and polygons) and relationships (i.e., non-Euclidean distances, direction, connectivity, and interaction through attributed geographic space such as terrain). Furthermore, the time dimension needs to be more fully integrated into these geographic representations and relationships.

- **Geographic knowledge discovery using diverse data types**: GKD methods should be developed that can handle diverse data types beyond the traditional raster and vector models, including imagery and geo-referenced multimedia, as well as dynamic data types (video streams, animation).

11.7   Temporal data mining

Data may contain attributes generated and recorded at different times. In this case finding meaningful relationships in the data may require considering the temporal order of the attributes. A temporal relationship may indicate a causal relationship, or simply an association.

11.8   Sensor data mining

Wireless sensor networks can be used for facilitating the collection of data for spatial data mining for a variety of applications such as air pollution monitoring.[32] A characteristic of such networks is that nearby sensor nodes monitoring an environmental feature typically register similar values. This kind of data redundancy due to the spatial correlation between sensor observations inspires the techniques for in-network data aggregation and mining. By measuring the spatial correlation between data sampled by different sensors, a wide class of specialized algorithms can be developed to develop more efficient spatial data mining algorithms.[33]

11.9   Visual data mining

In the process of turning from analogical into digital, large data sets have been generated, collected, and stored discovering statistical patterns, trends and information which is hidden in data, in order to build predictive patterns. Studies suggest visual data mining is faster and much more intuitive than is traditional data mining.[34][35][36] See also Computer vision.

11.10 Music data mining

Data mining techniques, and in particular co-occurrence analysis, has been used to discover relevant similarities among music corpora (radio lists, CD databases) for purposes including classifying music into genres in a more objective manner.[37]

11.11 Surveillance

Data mining has been used by the U.S. government. Programs include the Total Information Awareness (TIA) program, Secure Flight (formerly known as Computer-Assisted Passenger Prescreening System (CAPPS II)), Analysis, Dissemination, Visualization, Insight, Semantic Enhancement (ADVISE),[38] and the Multi-state Anti-Terrorism Information Exchange (MATRIX).[39] These programs have been discontinued due to controversy over whether they violate the 4th Amendment to the United States Constitution, although many programs that were formed under them continue to be funded by different organizations or under different names.[40]

In the context of combating terrorism, two particularly plausible methods of data mining are "pattern mining" and "subject-based data mining".

11.12 Pattern mining

"Pattern mining" is a data mining method that involves finding existing patterns in data. In this context *patterns* often means association rules. The original motivation for searching association rules came from the desire to analyze supermarket transaction data, that is, to examine customer behavior in terms of the purchased products. For example, an association rule "beer $\Rightarrow$ potato chips (80%)" states that four out of five customers that bought beer also bought potato chips.

In the context of pattern mining as a tool to identify terrorist activity, the National Research Council provides the following definition: "Pattern-based data mining looks for patterns (including anomalous data patterns) that might be associated with terrorist activity — these patterns might be regarded as small signals in a large ocean of noise."[41][42][43] Pattern Mining includes new areas such a Music Information Retrieval (MIR) where patterns seen both in the temporal and non temporal domains are imported to classical knowledge discovery search methods.

11.13 Subject-based data mining

"Subject-based data mining" is a data mining method involving the search for associations between individuals in data. In the context of combating terrorism, the National Research Council provides the following definition: "Subject-based data mining uses an initiating individual or other datum that is considered, based on other information, to be of high interest, and the goal is to determine what other persons or financial transactions or movements, etc., are related to that initiating datum."[42]

11.14 Knowledge grid

Knowledge discovery "On the Grid" generally refers to conducting knowledge discovery in an open environment using grid computing concepts, allowing users to integrate data from various online data sources, as well make use of remote resources, for executing their data mining tasks. The earliest example was the Discovery Net,[44][45] developed at Imperial College London, which won the "Most Innovative Data-Intensive Application Award" at the ACM SC02 (Supercomputing 2002) conference and exhibition, based on a demonstration of a fully interactive distributed knowledge discovery application for a bioinformatics application. Other examples include work conducted by researchers at the University of Calabria, who developed a Knowledge Grid architecture for distributed knowledge discovery, based on grid computing.[46][47]

11.15   References

[1] O'Brien, J. A., & Marakas, G. M. (2011). Management Information Systems. New York, NY: McGraw-Hill/Irwin.

[2] Alexander, D. (n.d.). Data Mining. Retrieved from The University of Texas at Austin: College of Liberal Arts: http://www. laits.utexas.edu/~{ }anorman/BUS.FOR/course.mat/Alex/

[3] "Daniele Medri: Big Data & Business: An on-going revolution". Statistics Views. 21 Oct 2013.

[4] "Large Scale Item Categorization" (PDF).

[5] Goss, S. (2013, April 10). Data-mining and our personal privacy. Retrieved from The Telegraph: http://www.macon.com/ 2013/04/10/2429775/data-mining-and-our-personal-privacy.html

[6] Monk, Ellen; Wagner, Bret (2006). *Concepts in Enterprise Resource Planning, Second Edition*. Boston, MA: Thomson Course Technology. ISBN 0-619-21663-8. OCLC 224465825.

[7] Elovici, Yuval; Braha, Dan (2003). "A Decision-Theoretic Approach to Data Mining" (PDF). *IEEE Transactions on Systems, Man, and Cybernetics—Part A: Systems and Humans* **33** (1).

[8] Battiti, Roberto; and Brunato, Mauro; *Reactive Business Intelligence. From Data to Models to Insight*, Reactive Search Srl, Italy, February 2011. ISBN 978-88-905795-0-9.

[9] Battiti, Roberto; Passerini, Andrea (2010). "Brain-Computer Evolutionary Multi-Objective Optimization (BC-EMO): a genetic algorithm adapting to the decision maker" (PDF). *IEEE Transactions on Evolutionary Computation* **14** (15): 671–687. doi:10.1109/TEVC.2010.2058118.

[10] Braha, Dan; Elovici, Yuval; Last, Mark (2007). "Theory of actionable data mining with application to semiconductor manufacturing control" (PDF). *International Journal of Production Research* **45** (13).

[11] Fountain, Tony; Dietterich, Thomas; and Sudyka, Bill (2000); *Mining IC Test Data to Optimize VLSI Testing*, in Proceedings of the Sixth ACM SIGKDD International Conference on Knowledge Discovery & Data Mining, ACM Press, pp. 18–25

[12] Braha, Dan; Shmilovici, Armin (2002). "Data Mining for Improving a Cleaning Process in the Semiconductor Industry" (PDF). *IEEE Transactions on Semiconductor Manufacturing* **15** (1).

[13] Braha, Dan; Shmilovici, Armin (2003). "On the Use of Decision Tree Induction for Discovery of Interactions in a Photolithographic Process" (PDF). *IEEE Transactions on Semiconductor Manufacturing* **16** (4).

[14] Zhu, Xingquan; Davidson, Ian (2007). *Knowledge Discovery and Data Mining: Challenges and Realities*. New York, NY: Hershey. p. 18. ISBN 978-1-59904-252-7.

[15] McGrail, Anthony J.; Gulski, Edward; Allan, David; Birtwhistle, David; Blackburn, Trevor R.; Groot, Edwin R. S. "Data Mining Techniques to Assess the Condition of High Voltage Electrical Plant". *CIGRÉ WG 15.11 of Study Committee 15*.

[16] Baker, Ryan S. J. d. "Is Gaming the System State-or-Trait? Educational Data Mining Through the Multi-Contextual Application of a Validated Behavioral Model". *Workshop on Data Mining for User Modeling 2007*.

[17] Superby Aguirre, Juan Francisco; Vandamme, Jean-Philippe; Meskens, Nadine. "Determination of factors influencing the achievement of the first-year university students using data mining methods". *Workshop on Educational Data Mining 2006*.

[18] Zhu, Xingquan; Davidson, Ian (2007). *Knowledge Discovery and Data Mining: Challenges and Realities*. New York, NY: Hershey. pp. 163–189. ISBN 978-1-59904-252-7.

[19] Zhu, Xingquan; Davidson, Ian (2007). *Knowledge Discovery and Data Mining: Challenges and Realities*. New York, NY: Hershey. pp. 31–48. ISBN 978-1-59904-252-7.

[20] Chen, Yudong; Zhang, Yi; Hu, Jianming; Li, Xiang (2006). "Traffic Data Analysis Using Kernel PCA and Self-Organizing Map". *IEEE Intelligent Vehicles Symposium*.

[21] Bate, Andrew; Lindquist, Marie; Edwards, I. Ralph; Olsson, Sten; Orre, Roland; Lansner, Anders; de Freitas, Rogelio Melhado (Jun 1998). "A Bayesian neural network method for adverse drug reaction signal generation" (PDF). *European Journal of Clinical Pharmacology* **54** (4): 315–21. doi:10.1007/s002280050466. PMID 9696956.

[22] Norén, G. Niklas; Bate, Andrew; Hopstadius, Johan; Star, Kristina; and Edwards, I. Ralph (2008); Temporal Pattern Discovery for Trends and Transient Effects: Its Application to Patient Records. *Proceedings of the Fourteenth International Conference on Knowledge Discovery and Data Mining (SIGKDD 2008), Las Vegas, NV*, pp. 963–971.

[23] Zernik, Joseph; Data Mining as a Civic Duty – Online Public Prisoners' Registration Systems, *International Journal on Social Media: Monitoring, Measurement, Mining*, 1: 84–96 (2010)

[24] Zernik, Joseph; Data Mining of Online Judicial Records of the Networked US Federal Courts, *International Journal on Social Media: Monitoring, Measurement, Mining*, 1:69–83 (2010)

[25] Gagliardi, F (2011). "Instance-based classifiers applied to medical databases: Diagnosis and knowledge extraction". *Artificial Intelligence in Medicine* **52** (3): 123–139. doi:10.1016/j.artmed.2011.04.002.

[26] David G. Savage (2011-06-24). "Pharmaceutical industry: Supreme Court sides with pharmaceutical industry in two decisions". *Los Angeles Times*. Retrieved 2012-11-07.

[27] Analyzing Medical Data. (2012). *Communications of the ACM* 55(6), 13-15. doi:10.1145/2184319.2184324

[28] http://searchhealthit.techtarget.com/definition/HITECH-Act

[29] Healey, Richard G. (1991); *Database Management Systems*, in Maguire, David J.; Goodchild, Michael F.; and Rhind, David W., (eds.), *Geographic Information Systems: Principles and Applications*, London, GB: Longman

[30] Camara, Antonio S.; and Raper, Jonathan (eds.) (1999); *Spatial Multimedia and Virtual Reality*, London, GB: Taylor and Francis

[31] Miller, Harvey J.; and Han, Jiawei (eds.) (2001); *Geographic Data Mining and Knowledge Discovery*, London, GB: Taylor & Francis

[32] Ma, Y.; Richards, M.; Ghanem, M.; Guo, Y.; Hassard, J. (2008). "Air Pollution Monitoring and Mining Based on Sensor Grid in London". *Sensors* **8** (6): 3601. doi:10.3390/s8063601.

[33] Ma, Y.; Guo, Y.; Tian, X.; Ghanem, M. (2011). "Distributed Clustering-Based Aggregation Algorithm for Spatial Correlated Sensor Networks". *IEEE Sensors Journal* **11** (3): 641. doi:10.1109/JSEN.2010.2056916.

[34] Zhao, Kaidi; and Liu, Bing; Tirpark, Thomas M.; and Weimin, Xiao; *A Visual Data Mining Framework for Convenient Identification of Useful Knowledge*

[35] Keim, Daniel A.; *Information Visualization and Visual Data Mining*

[36] Burch, Michael; Diehl, Stephan; Weißgerber, Peter; *Visual Data Mining in Software Archives*

[37] Pachet, François; Westermann, Gert; and Laigre, Damien; *Musical Data Mining for Electronic Music Distribution*, Proceedings of the 1st WedelMusic Conference,Firenze, Italy, 2001, pp. 101–106.

[38] Government Accountability Office, *Data Mining: Early Attention to Privacy in Developing a Key DHS Program Could Reduce Risks*, GAO-07-293 (February 2007), Washington, DC

[39] Secure Flight Program report, MSNBC

[40] "Total/Terrorism Information Awareness (TIA): Is It Truly Dead?". *Electronic Frontier Foundation (official website)*. 2003. Retrieved 2009-03-15.

[41] Agrawal, Rakesh; Mannila, Heikki; Srikant, Ramakrishnan; Toivonen, Hannu; and Verkamo, A. Inkeri; *Fast discovery of association rules*, in *Advances in knowledge discovery and data mining*, MIT Press, 1996, pp. 307–328

[42] National Research Council, *Protecting Individual Privacy in the Struggle Against Terrorists: A Framework for Program Assessment*, Washington, DC: National Academies Press, 2008

[43] Haag, Stephen; Cummings, Maeve; Phillips, Amy (2006). *Management Information Systems for the information age*. Toronto: McGraw-Hill Ryerson. p. 28. ISBN 0-07-095569-7. OCLC 63194770.

[44] Ghanem, Moustafa; Guo, Yike; Rowe, Anthony; Wendel, Patrick (2002). "Grid-based knowledge discovery services for high throughput informatics". *Proceedings 11th IEEE International Symposium on High Performance Distributed Computing*. p. 416. doi:10.1109/HPDC.2002.1029946. ISBN 0-7695-1686-6.

[45] Ghanem, Moustafa; Curcin, Vasa; Wendel, Patrick; Guo, Yike (2009). "Building and Using Analytical Workflows in Discovery Net". *Data Mining Techniques in Grid Computing Environments*. p. 119. doi:10.1002/9780470699904.ch8. ISBN 9780470699904.

[46] Cannataro, Mario; Talia, Domenico (January 2003). "The Knowledge Grid: An Architecture for Distributed Knowledge Discovery" (PDF). *Communications of the ACM* **46** (1): 89–93. doi:10.1145/602421.602425. Retrieved 17 October 2011.

[47] Talia, Domenico; Trunfio, Paolo (July 2010). "How distributed data mining tasks can thrive as knowledge services" (PDF). *Communications of the ACM* **53** (7): 132–137. doi:10.1145/1785414.1785451. Retrieved 17 October 2011.

Chapter 12

Human genetic clustering

Human genetic clustering analysis uses mathematical cluster analysis of the degree of similarity of genetic data between individuals and groups in order to infer population structures and assign individuals to groups. These groupings in turn often, but not always, correspond with the individuals' self-identified geographical ancestry. A similar analysis can be done using principal components analysis, which in earlier research was a popular method.[1] Many studies in the past few years have continued using principal components analysis.

12.1 Studies

12.1.1 Clusters by Rosenberg et al. (2006)

Main article: Race and genetics

In 2004, Lynn Jorde and Steven Wooding argued that "Analysis of many loci now yields reasonably accurate estimates of genetic similarity among individuals, rather than populations. Clustering of individuals is correlated with geographic origin or ancestry."[2]

Studies such as those by Risch and Rosenberg use a computer program called STRUCTURE to find human populations (gene clusters). It is a statistical program that works by placing individuals into one of an arbitrary number of clusters based on their overall genetic similarity, many possible pairs of clusters are tested per individual to generate multiple clusters.[3] These populations are based on multiple genetic markers that are often shared between different human populations even over large geographic ranges. The notion of a genetic cluster is that people within the cluster share on average similar allele frequencies to each other than to those in other clusters. (A. W. F. Edwards, 2003 but see also infobox "Multi Locus Allele Clusters") In a test of idealised populations, the computer programme STRUCTURE was found to consistently underestimate the numbers of populations in the data set when high migration rates between populations and slow mutation rates (such as single-nucleotide polymorphisms) were considered.[4]

Nevertheless the Rosenberg *et al.* (2002) paper shows that individuals can be assigned to specific clusters to a high degree of accuracy. One of the underlying questions regarding the distribution of human genetic diversity is related to the degree to which genes are shared between the observed clusters. It has been observed repeatedly that the majority of variation observed in the global human population is found within populations. This variation is usually calculated using Sewall Wright's Fixation index (FST), which is an estimate of between to within group variation. The degree of human genetic variation is a little different depending upon the gene type studied, but in general it is common to claim that ~85% of genetic variation is found within groups, ~6–10% between groups within the same continent and ~6–10% is found between continental groups. For example The Human Genome Project states "two random individuals from any one group are almost as different [genetically] as any two random individuals from the entire world."[5] Sarich and Miele, however, have argued that estimates of genetic difference between individuals of different populations fail to take into account human diploidity.

The point is that we are diploid organisms, getting one set of chromosomes from one parent and a second from the other. To the extent that your mother and father are not especially closely related, then, those two sets of chromosomes will come close to being a random sample of the chromosomes in your population. And the sets present in some randomly chosen member of yours will also be about as different from your two sets as they are from one another. So how much of the variability will be distributed where?

First is the 15 percent that is interpopulational. The other 85 percent will then split half and half (42.5 percent) between the intra- and interindividual within-population comparisons. The increase in variability in between-population comparisons is thus 15 percent against the 42.5 percent that is between-individual within-population. Thus, 15/42.5 is 32.5 percent, a much more impressive and, more important, more legitimate value than 15 percent.[6]

Additionally, Edwards (2003) claims in his essay "Lewontin's Fallacy" that: "It is not true, as *Nature* claimed, that 'two random individuals from any one group are almost as different as any two random individuals from the entire world'" and Risch *et al.* (2002) state "Two Caucasians are more similar to each other genetically than a Caucasian and an Asian." It should be noted that these statements are not the same. Risch *et al.* simply state that two indigenous individuals from the same geographical region are more similar to each other than either is to an indigenous individual from a different geographical region, a claim few would argue with. Jorde et al. put it like this:

> The picture that begins to emerge from this and other analyses of human genetic variation is that variation tends to be geographically structured, such that most individuals from the same geographic region will be more similar to one another than to individuals from a distant region.[2]

Whereas Edwards claims that it is not true that the differences between individuals from different geographical regions represent only a small proportion of the variation within the human population (he claims that within group differences between individuals are not almost as large as between group differences). Bamshad *et al.* (2004) used the data from Rosenberg *et al.* (2002) to investigate the extent of genetic differences between individuals within continental groups relative to genetic differences between individuals between continental groups. They found that though these individuals could be classified very accurately to continental clusters, there was a significant degree of genetic overlap on the individual level, to the extent that, using 377 loci, individual Europeans were about 38% of the time more genetically similar to East Asians than to other Europeans.

A study by the HUGO Pan-Asian SNP Consortium in 2009 using the similar principal components analysis found that East Asian and South-East Asian populations clustered together, and suggested a common origin for these populations. At the same time they observed a broad discontinuity between this cluster and South Asia, commenting "most of the Indian populations showed evidence of shared ancestry with European populations". It was noted that "genetic ancestry is strongly correlated with linguistic affiliations as well as geography".[7]

Criticism

The Rosenberg study has been criticised on several grounds.

The existence of allelic clines and the observation that the bulk of human variation is continuously distributed, has led some scientists to conclude that any categorization schema attempting to partition that variation meaningfully will necessarily create artificial truncations. (Kittles & Weiss 2003). It is for this reason, Reanne Frank argues, that attempts to allocate individuals into ancestry groupings based on genetic information have yielded varying results that are highly dependent on methodological design.[8] Serre and Pääbo (2004) make a similar claim:

> The absence of strong continental clustering in the human gene pool is of practical importance. It has recently been claimed that "the greatest genetic structure that exists in the human population occurs at the racial level" (Risch et al. 2002). Our results show that this is not the case, and we see no reason to assume that "races" represent any units of relevance for understanding human genetic history.

In a response to Serre and Pääbo (2004), Rosenberg *et al.* (2005) make three relevant observations. Firstly they maintain that their clustering analysis is robust. Secondly they agree with Serre and Pääbo that membership of multiple clusters can be interpreted as evidence for clinality (isolation by distance), though they also comment that this may also be due to admixture between neighbouring groups (small island model). Thirdly they comment that evidence of clusterdness is not evidence for any concepts of "biological race".[9]

Risch *et al.* (2002) state that "two Caucasians are more similar to each other genetically than a Caucasian and an Asian", but Bamshad *et al.* (2004)[10] used the same data set as Rosenberg *et al.* (2002) to show that Europeans are more similar to Asians 38% of the time than they are to other Europeans when only 377 microsatellite markers are analysed.

In agreement with the observation of Bamshad *et al.* (2004), Witherspoon *et al.* (2007) have shown that many more than 326 or 377 microsatellite loci are required in order to show that individuals are always more similar to individuals in their own population group than to individuals in different population groups, even for three distinct populations.[5]

Witherspoon et al. (2007) have argued that even when individuals can be reliably assigned to specific population groups, it may still be possible for two randomly chosen individuals from different populations/clusters to be more similar to each other than to a randomly chosen member of their own cluster. They found that many thousands of genetic markers had to be used in order for the answer to the question "How often is a pair of individuals from one population genetically more dissimilar than two individuals chosen from two different populations?" to be "never". This assumed three population groups separated by large geographic ranges (European, African and East Asian). The entire world population is much more complex and studying an increasing number of groups would require an increasing number of markers for the same answer. Witherspoon et al. conclude that "caution should be used when using geographic or genetic ancestry to make inferences about individual phenotypes."

Clustering does not particularly correspond to continental divisions. Depending on the parameters given to their analytical program, Rosenberg and Pritchard were able to construct between divisions of between 4 and 20 clusters of the genomes studied, although they excluded analysis with more than 6 clusters from their published article. Probability values for various cluster configurations varied widely, with the single most likely configuration coming with 16 clusters although other 16-cluster configurations had low probabilities. Overall, "there is no clear evidence that K=6 was the best estimate" according to geneticist Deborah Bolnick (2008:76-77).[12] The number of genetic clusters used in the study was arbitrarily chosen. Although the original research used different number of clusters, the published study emphasized six genetic clusters. The number of genetic clusters is determined by the user of the computer software conducting the study. Rosenberg later revealed that his team used pre-conceived numbers of genetic clusters from six to twenty "but did not publish those results because Structure [the computer program used] identified multiple ways to divide the sampled individuals". Dorothy Roberts, a law professor, asserts that "there is nothing in the team's findings that suggests that six clusters represent human population structure better than ten, or fifteen, or twenty."[13] When instructed to find two clusters, the program identified two populations anchored around by Africa and by the Americas. In the case of six clusters, the entirety of Kalesh people, an ethnic group living in Northern Pakistan, was added to the previous five.[14][15]

The law professor, Dorothy Roberts asserts that "the study actually showed that there are many ways to slice the expansive range of human genetic variation. In a 2005 paper, Rosenberg and his team acknowledged that findings of a study on human population structure are highly influenced by the way the study is designed.[15][16]

They reported that the number of loci, the sample size, the geographic dispersion of the samples and assumptions about allele-frequency correlation all have an effect on the outcome of the study. Rosenberg stated that their findings "should not be taken as evidence of our support of any particular concept of biological race (...). Genetic differences among human populations derive mainly from gradations in allele frequencies rather than from distinctive 'diagnostic' genotypes."[17] The study's overall results confirmed that genetic difference within populations is between 93 and 95%. Only 5% of genetic variation is found between groups.[15]

12.2 Controversy of genetic clustering and associations with "race"

In the late 1990s Harvard evolutionary geneticist Richard Lewontin stated that "no justification can be offered for continuing the biological concept of race. (...) Genetic data shows that no matter how racial groups are defined, two people from the same racial group are about as different from each other as two people from any two different racial groups.[18]

Lewontin's statement came under attack when new genomic technologies permitted the analysis of gene clusters. In 2003,

British statistician and evolutionary biologist A. W. F. Edwards faulted Lewontin's statement for basing his conclusions on simple comparison of genes and rather on a more complex structure of gene frequencies. Edwards charged Lewontin that he made an "unjustified assault on human classification, which he deplored for social reasons."[19]

According to Roberts, "Edwards did not refute Lewontin's claim: that there is more genetic variation within populations than between them, especially when it comes to races. (...) Lewontin did not ignore biology to support his social ideology (...). To the contrary, he argued that there is no biological support for the ideological project of race." "The genetic differences that exist among populations are characterized by gradual changes across geographic regions, not sharp, categorical distinctions. Groups of people across the globe have varying frequencies of polymorphic genes, which are genes with any of several differing nucleotide sequences. There is no such thing as a set of genes that belongs exclusively to one group and not to another. The clinal, gradually changing nature of geographic genetic difference is complicated further by the migration and mixing that human groups have engaged in since prehistoric times. Race [however defined] collapses infinite diversity into a few discrete categories that in reality cannot be demarcated genetically."[15]

Genetic clustering was also criticized by Penn State anthropologists Kenneth Weiss and Brian Lambert. They asserted that understanding human population structure in terms of discrete genetic clusters misrepresents the path that produced diverse human populations that diverged from shared ancestors in Africa. Ironically, by ignoring the way population history actually works as one process from a common origin rather than as a string of creation events, structure analysis that seems to present variation in Darwinian evolutionary terms is fundamentally non-Darwinian."[20]

In 2006, Lewontin wrote that any genetic study requires some priori concept of race or ethnicity in order to package human genetic diversity into defined, limited number of biological groupings. Informed by geneticist, zoologists have long discarded the concept of race for dividing up groups of non-human animal populations within a species. Defined on varying criteria, in the same species widely varying number of races could be distinguished. Lewontin notes that genetic testing revealed that "because so many of these races turned out to be based on only one or two genes, two animals born in the same litter could belong to different 'races'".[21]

Studies that seek to find genetic clusters are only as informative as the populations they sample. For example Risch and Burchard relied on two or three local populations from five continents, which together were supposed to represent the entire human race.[15] Another genetic clustering study used three sub-Saharan population groups to represent Africa; Chinese, Japanese, and Cambodian samples for East Asia; Northern European and Northern Italian samples to represent "Caucasians". Entire regions, subcontinents, and landmasses are left out of many studies. Furthermore, social geographical categories such "East Asia" and "Caucasians" were not defined. "A handful of ethnic groups to symbolize an entire continent mimic a basic tenet of racial thinking: that because races are composed of uniform individuals, anyone can represent the whole group" notes Roberts.[15][22][23]

The model of Big Few fails when including overlooked geographical regions such as India. The 2003 study which examined fifty-eight genetic markers found that Indian populations had their ancestral lineages to Africa, Central Asia, Europe, and southern China.[24][25] Reardon, from Princeton University, asserts that flawed sampling methods are built into many genetic research projects. The Human Genome Diversity Project (HGDP) relied on samples which were assumed to be geographically separate and isolated.[26] The relatively small sample sizes of indigenous populations for the HGDP do not represent the human species' genetic diversity, nor do they portray migrations and mixing population groups which has been happening since prehistoric times. Geographic areas such as the Balkans, the Middle East, North and East Africa, and Spain are seldom included in genetic studies.[15][27] East and North African indigenous populations, for example, are never selected to represent Africa because they do not fit the profile of "black" Africa. The sampled indigenous populations of the HGDP are assumed to be "pure"; the law professor Roberts claims that "their unusual purity is all the more reason they cannot stand in for all the other populations of the world that marked by intermixture from migration, commerce, and conquest."[15]

King and Motulsky, in a 2002 Science article, states that "While the computer-generated findings from all of these studies offer greater insight into the genetic unity and diversity of the human species, as well as its ancient migratory history, none support dividing the species into discrete, genetically determined racial categories".[28] Cavalli-Sforza asserts that classifying clusters as races would be a "futile exercise" because "every level of clustering would determine a different population and there is no biological reason to prefer a particular one." Bamshad, in 2004 paper published in Nature, asserts that a more accurate study of human genetic variation would use an objective sampling method. An objective sampling method would chose populations randomly and systematically across the world, including those populations which are characterized by historical intermingling, instead of cherry-picking population samples which fit a priori concept of racial classification. Roberts states that "if research collected DNA samples continuously from region to region throughout the world, they would find it impossible to infer neat boundaries between large geographical groups."[10][15][29][30]

Anthropologists such as C. Loring Brace,[31] philosophers Jonathan Kaplan and Rasmus Winther,[32][33][34][35] and geneticist Joseph Graves,[36] have argued that while there it is certainly possible to find biological and genetic variation that corresponds roughly to the groupings normally defined as "continental races", this is true for almost all geographically distinct populations. The cluster structure of the genetic data is therefore dependent on the initial hypotheses of the researcher and the populations sampled. When one samples continental groups the clusters become continental, if one had chosen other sampling patterns the clustering would be different. Weiss and Fullerton have noted that if one sampled only Icelanders, Mayans and Maoris, three distinct clusters would form and all other populations could be described as being clinally composed of admixtures of Maori, Icelandic and Mayan genetic materials.[37] Kaplan and Winther therefore argue that seen in this way both Lewontin and Edwards are right in their arguments. They conclude that while racial groups are characterized by different allele frequencies, this does not mean that racial classification is a natural taxonomy of the human species, because multiple other genetic patterns can be found in human populations that crosscut racial distinctions. Moreover, the genomic data underdetermines whether one wishes to see subdivisions (i.e., splitters) or a continuum (i.e., lumpers). Under Kaplan and Winther's view, racial groupings are objective social constructions (see Mills 1998 [38]) that have conventional biological reality only insofar as the categories are chosen and constructed for pragmatic scientific reasons.

12.2.1 Commercial ancestry testing and individual ancestry

Commercial ancestry testing companies, who use genetic clustering data, have been also heavily criticized. Limitations of genetic clustering are intensified when inferred population structure is applied to individual ancestry. The type of statistical analysis conducted by scientists translates poorly into individual ancestry because they are looking at difference in frequencies, not absolute differences between groups. Commercial genetic genealogy companies are guilty of what Pillar Ossorio calls the "tendency to transform statistical claims into categorical ones".[39] Not just individuals of the same local ethnic group, but two siblings may end up beings as members of different continental groups or "races" depending on the alleles they inherit.[15]

Many commercial companies use data from HapMap's initial phrase, where population samples were collected from four ethnic groups in the world: Han Chinese, Japanese, Yoruba Nigerian, and Utah residents of Northern European ancestry. If a person has ancestry from a region where the computer program does not have samples, it will compensate with the closest sample that may have nothing to do with the customer's actual ancestry: "Consider a genetic ancestry testing performed on an individual we will call Joe, whose eight great-grandparents were from southern Europe. The HapMap populations are used as references for testing Joe's genetic ancestry. The HapMap's European samples consist of "northern" Europeans. In regions of Joe's genome that vary between northern and southern Europe (such regions might include the lactase gene), the genetic ancestry test is using the HapMap reference population is likely to incorrectly assign the ancestry of that portion of the genome to a non-European population because that genomic region will appear to be more similar to the HapMap's Yoruba or Han Chinese samples than to Northern European samples.[40] Likewise, a person with East African ancestors may be classified as someone having part North European and part Western African ancestry.[41] "Telling customers that they are a composite of several anthropological groupings reinforces three central myths about race: that there are pure races, that each race contains people who are fundamentally the same and fundamentally different from people in other races, and that races can be biologically demarcated." Many companies base their findings on inadequate and unscientific sampling methods. Researchers have never sampled the world's populations in a systematic and random fashion.[15]

12.2.2 Geographical and continental groupings

Roberts argues against the use of broad geographical or continental groupings: "molecular geneticists routinely refer to African ancestry as if everyone on the continent is more similar to each other than they are to people of other continents, who may be closer both geographically and genetically.[15] Ethiopians have closer genetic affinity with Armenians and Norwegians than with Bantu populations.[42] Similarly, Somalis are genetically more similar to Gulf Arab populations than to other populations in Africa.[43] Braun and Hammonds (2008) asserts that the misperception of continents as natural population groupings is rooted in the assumption that populations are natural, isolated, and static. Populations came to be seen as "bounded units amenable to scientific sampling, analysis, and classification".[44] Human beings are not naturally organized into definable, genetically cohesive populations.

12.2.3 Usage in scientific journals

Some scientific journals have addressed previous methodological errors by requiring more rigorous scrutiny of population variables. Since 2000, Nature Genetics requires its authors to "explain why they make use of particular ethnic groups or populations, and how classification was achieved." Editors of Nature Genetics say that "[they] hope that this will raise awareness and inspire more rigorous design of genetic and epidemiological studies."[45] Nature later released an article stating that race is social and not a biological unit in the human species. In contrast to chimpanzees, the human species does not have races or subspecies.[46]

12.3 See also

- Haplogroup

- Human genetic variation

- Gene cluster

- Genetic admixture

- Population groups in biomedicine

- Y-chromosome haplogroups by populations

12.4 References

[1] Patterson, Nick; Price, Alkes L.; Reich, David. "Population Structure and Eigenanalysis". *PLoS Genet* **2** (12): e190. doi:10.1371/journal.pgen.00201

[2] Lynn B Jorde & Stephen P Wooding, 2004, "Genetic variation, classification and 'race'" in *Nature Genetics* 36, S28–S33 Genetic variation, classification and 'race'

[3] "Genetic Similarities Within and Between Human Populations" (2007) by D.J. Witherspoon, S. Wooding, A.R. Rogers, E.E. Marchani, W.S. Watkins, M.A. Batzer and L.B. Jorde. *Genetics.* **176**(1) 351–359.

[4] Wapples, R., S. and Gaggiotti, O. *What is a population? An empirical evaluation of some genetic methods for identifying the number of gene pools and their degree of connectivity Molecular Ecology* (2006) **15:** 1419–1439. doi:10.1111/j.1365-294X.2006.02890.x PMID 16629801

[5] *Genetic Similarities Within and Between Human Populations* by D. J. Witherspoon, S. Wooding, A. R. Rogers, E. E. Marchani, W. S. Watkins, M. A. Batzer, and L. B. Jorde Genetics. 2007 May; 176(1): 351–359.

[6] Sarich VM, Miele F. Race: The Reality of Human Differences. Westview Press (2004). ISBN 0-8133-4086-1

[7] Mapping Human Genetic Diversity in Asia, The HUGO Pan-Asian SNP Consortium, 2009

[8] Back with a Vengeance: the Reemergence of a Biological Conceptualization of Race in Research on Race/Ethnic Disparities in Health Reanne Frank

[9] *Rosenberg NA, Mahajan S, Ramachandran S, Zhao C, Pritchard JK,* et al. *(2005)* Clines, Clusters, and the Effect of Study Design on the Inference of Human Population Structure. PLoS Genet *1(6): e70 doi:10.1371/journal.pgen.0010070 PMID 16355252*

[10] Michael Bamshad; et al. (2004). "Deconstructing the Relationship Between Genetics and Race". *Nature Reviews Genetics* **5** (598): 598–609. doi:10.1038/nrg1401. PMID 15266342.

[11] The table gives the percentage likelihood that two individuals from different clusters are genetically more similar to each other than to someone from their own population when 377 microsatellite markers are considered from Michael Bamshad; et al. (2004). "Deconstructing the Relationship Between Genetics and Race". *Nature Reviews Genetics* **5** (598): 598–609. doi:10.1038/nrg1401. PMID 15266342., original data from Rosenberg (2002).

[12] Bolnick, Deborah A. (2008). "Individual Ancestry Inference and the Reification of Race as a Biological Phenomenon". In Koenig, Barbara A.; Richardson, Sarah S.; Lee, Sandra Soo-Jin. *Revisiting race in a genomic age*. Rutgers University Press. ISBN 978-0-8135-4324-6.

[13] Kalinowski. "The Computer Program STRUCTURE Does Not Reliably Identify Main Genetic Clusters Within Species" **4**. pp. 67–77.

[14] Sadaf Firasat, Shagufta Khalig, Aisha Mohyuddin, Myrto papioannou, Chris Tyler-Smith, Peter A. Underhill, and Qasim Ayub (2007). "Y-Chromosomal Evidence for a Limited Greek Contribution to the Pathan Population of Pakistan". *European Journal of Human Genetics* **15**: 121–6. doi:10.1038/sj.ejhg.5201726. PMC 2588664. PMID 17047675.

[15] Roberts, Dorothy (2011). *Fatal Invention*. London, New York: The New Press.

[16] Noah A. Rosenberg, Saurabh Mahajan, Sohini Ramachandran, Chengfeng Zhao, Jonathan K. Pritchard, and Marcus Feldman (2005). "Clines, Clusters, and the Effects of Study Design on the Inference of Human Population Science". *PloS Genetics* **1**: 660, 668. doi:10.1371/journal.pgen.0010070. PMC 1310579. PMID 16355252.

[17] Rosenberg; et al. "Genetic Structure of Human Populations". p. 2384.

[18] "Response to OMB Directive 15". American Anthropological Association. 1997.

[19] A.W.F. Edwards (2003). "Human Genetic Diversity: Lewontin's Fallacy". *BioEssays* **25** (8): 798–801. doi:10.1002/bies.10315. PMID 12879450.

[20] Kenneth M. Weiss and Brian W. Lambert (2010). "Does History Matter? Do the Facts of Human Variation Package Our Views or Do Our Views Package the Facts?". *Evolutionary Anthropology* **19**: 92, 97. doi:10.1002/evan.20261.

[21] "Confusion About Human Races". Social Science Research Council. 26 July 2006.

[22] Charles N. Rotini and Lynn B. Jorde (2010). "Ancestry and Disease in the Age of Genomic Medicine". *New England Journal of Medicine* **363**: 1551–1552. doi:10.1056/nejmra0911564.

[23] S.O.Y. Keita and Rick A. Kittles (1997). "The Persistence of Racial Thinking and the Myth of Racial Divergence". *American Anthropologist* **99**: 534–544. doi:10.1525/aa.1997.99.3.534.

[24] Rick A. Kittles and Kenneth M. Wells (2003). "Race, Ancestry, and Genes: Implications for Defining Disease Risk". *Annual Review of Genomics and Human Genetics* **4**: 33, 38. doi:10.1146/annurev.genom.4.070802.110356. PMID 14527296.

[25] Analabha Basul; et al. (2003). "Ethnic India: A Genomic View with Special Reference to Peopling and Structure". *Genome Research* **13** (10): 2277–90. doi:10.1101/gr.1413403. PMC 403703. PMID 14525929.

[26] Reardon, Jenny (2005). *Race to the Finish: Identity and Governance in the Age of Genomics*. Princeton, NJ: Princeton University Press.

[27] Graves, Joseph (2004). *The Race Myth*. New York: Dutton. p. 113.

[28] Mary-Claire King and Arno G. Motulsky (2002). "Mapping Human History". *Science* **298** (5602): 2342–2343. doi:10.1126/science.1080373

[29] John H. Fujimura, Ramya Rajagopalan, Pilar N. Ossorio, and Kjell A. Doksum (2010). "Race and Ancestry: Operationalizing Populations in Human Genetic Variation Studies". *What's the Use of Race? Modern Governance and the Biology of Difference* (Cambridge MIT Press).

[30] L. Luca Cavalli-Sforza, Paolo Menozzi and Alberto Piazza (1994). *The History and Geography of Human Genes*. Princeton, NJ: Princeton University Press.

[31] Loring Brace, C. 2005. Race is a four letter word. Oxford University Press.

[32] Kaplan, Jonathan Michael (January 2011) 'Race': What Biology Can Tell Us about a Social Construct. In: Encyclopedia of Life Sciences (ELS). John Wiley & Sons, Ltd: Chichester

[33] Kaplan, Jonathan Michael (January 2011) 'Race': What Biology Can Tell Us about a Social Construct. In: Encyclopedia of Life Sciences (ELS). John Wiley & Sons, Ltd: Chichester

[34] Winther, Rasmus Grønfeldt (2011) ¿La cosificación genética de la 'raza'? Un análisis crítico in C López-Beltrán (ed.) *Genes (&) Mestizos. Genómica y raza en la biomedicina mexicana.* Ficticia editorial http://philpapers.org/archive/WINLCG.1.pdf

[35] Kaplan, Jonathan Michael, Winther, Rasmus Grønfeldt (2012). Prisoners of Abstraction? The Theory and Measure of Genetic Variation, and the Very Concept of 'Race' *Biological Theory* 7 http://philpapers.org/archive/KAPPOA.14.pdf

[36] Graves, Joseph. 2001. The Emperor's New Clothes. Rutgers University Press

[37] Weiss KM and Fullerton SM (2005) Racing around, getting nowhere. Evolutionary Anthropology 14: 165–169

[38] Mills CW (1988) "But What Are You Really? The Metaphysics of Race" in *Blackness visible: essays on philosophy and race*, pp. 41-66. Cornell University Press, Ithaca, NY

[39] Pillar Ossorio (2005). "Race, Genetic Variation, and the Haplotype Mapping Project". *Louisiana Law Review* **66** (131, 141).

[40] Royal, Novembre, Fullerton; et al. "Inferring Genetic Ancestry" (667-68).

[41] Mark D., Shriver; Rick A. Kittles (2004). "Genetic Ancestry and the Search for Personalized Genetic Histories". *Nature Reviews Genetics* **5**: 611–8. doi:10.1038/nrg1405. PMID 15266343.

[42] Wilson, James F.; Weale, Michael E.; Smith, Alice C.; Gratrix, Fiona; Fletcher, Benjamin; Thomas, Mark G.; Bradman, Neil; Goldstein, David B. (2001). "Population genetic structure of variable drug response". *Nature Genetics* **29** (3): 265–9. doi:10.1038/ng761. PMID 11685208.

[43] Mohamoud, A. M. (October 2006). "P52 Characteristics of HLA Class I and Class II Antigens of the Somali Population". *Transfusion Medicine* **16** (Supplement s1): 47. doi:10.1111/j.1365-3148.2006.00694_52.x.

[44] Braun, Lundy; Evelynn Hammonds (2008). "Race, Populations, and Genomics: Africa as Laboratory". *Social Science & Medicine* **67**: 1580–8. doi:10.1016/j.socscimed.2008.07.018.

[45] "Census, Race and Science". *Nature Genetics* **24** (2): 97–98. 2000. doi:10.1038/72884.

[46] S.O.Y. Keita, R. A. Kittles, C. D. M. Royal, G. E. Bonney, P. Furbert-Harris, G. M. Dunston, and C. N. Rotimi (November 2004). "Conceptualizing human variation". *Nature Genetics* **36**: S17–20. doi:10.1038/ng1455. PMID 15507998. Retrieved 18 March 2013.

Bantu (S. Africa)
Bantu (Kenya)
Mandenka
Yoruba
San
Mbuti Pygmy
Biaka Pygmy
Orcadian
Adygei
Russian
Basque
French
Italian
Sardinian
Tuscan
Mozabite

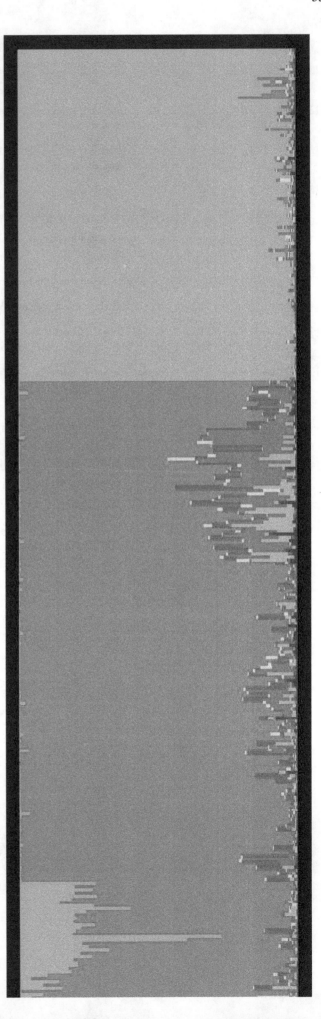

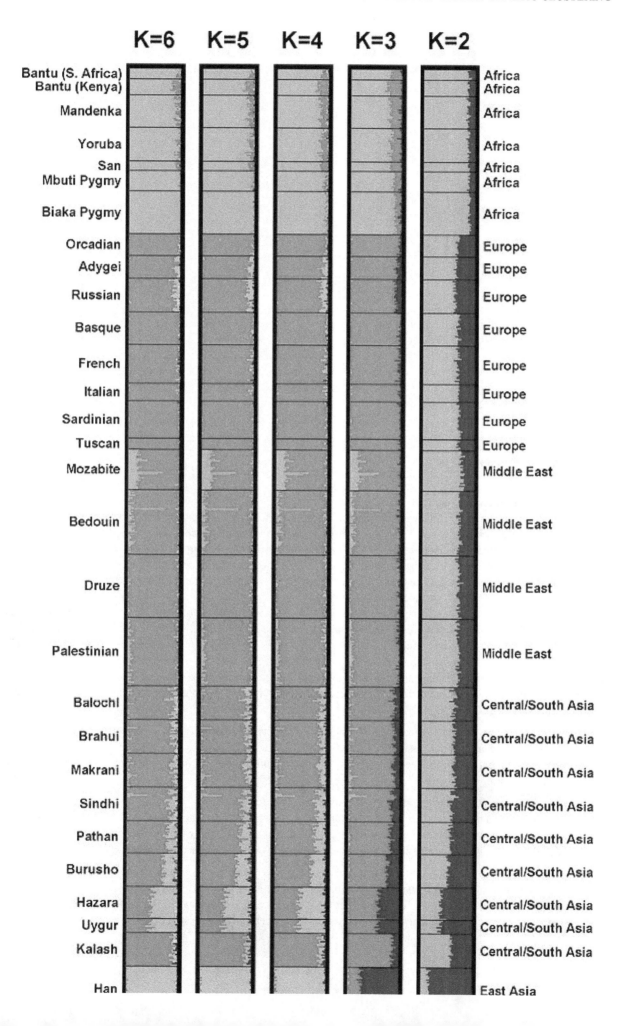

Chapter 13

Inference attack

An **Inference Attack** is a data mining technique performed by analyzing data in order to illegitimately gain knowledge about a subject or database.[1] A subject's sensitive information can be considered as leaked if an adversary can infer its real value with a high confidence.[2] This is an example of breached information security. An Inference attack occurs when a user is able to infer from trivial information more robust information about a database without directly accessing it.[3] The object of Inference attacks is to piece together information at one security level to determine a fact that should be protected at a higher security level.[4]

13.1 Countermeasures

Computer security inference control is the attempt to prevent users to infer classified information from rightfully accessible chunks of information with lower classification. Computer security professionals install protocols into databases to prevent inference attacks by software. Techniques to detect and remove inference channels can be organized into two categories. The first category includes techniques that detect inference channels during database design time. Inference channels are removed by modifying the database design or by increasing the classification levels of some of the data items. Techniques in the second category seek to eliminate inference channel violations during query processing time. If an inference channel is detected, the query is either refused or modified to avoid security violations. While design-time is easier to manage and implement, query-time approach allows more availability of data than in design-time approach because more information (past and present queries/answers) can be used for disclosure inference. Disclosure Monitor (DiMon) detects and eliminates inference channels based on database constraints. A Disclosure Inference Engine (DiIE) is proposed, that generates all information that can be disclosed based on a user's previous query results, the current query results, and a set of Horn-clause constraints. Dynamic Disclosure Monitor (D2Mon) guarantees data confidentiality and maximal availability even in the presence of inferences and updates. It is our intention to complement an existing access control mechanism (e.g., DAC, MAC, RBAC) to address the inference problem.

MAC: In the Mandatory Access Control (MAC) model, users are given permissions to resources by an administrator. Only an administrator can grant permissions or right to objects and resources. Access to resources is based on an object's security level, while users are granted security clearance. Only administrators can modify an object's security label or a user's security clearance.

DAC: In the Discretionary Access Control (DAC) model, access to resources is based on user's identity. A user is granted permissions to a resource by being placed on an access control list (ACL) associated with resource. An entry on a resource's ACL is known as an Access Control Entry (ACE). When a user (or group) is the owner of an object in the DAC model, the user can grant permission to other users and groups. The DAC model is based on resource ownership.

RBAC: In the Role-Based Access Control (RBAC) model, access to resources is based on the role assigned to a user. In this model, an administrator assigns a user to a role that has certain predetermined right and privileges. Because of the user's association with the role, the user can access certain resources and perform specific tasks. RBAC is also known as Non-Discretionary Access Control. The roles assigned to users are centrally administered. Dynamic Disclosure Monitor

Architecture uses this MAC to detect any direct security violation, if any direct security violation is detected the query is rejected then and there, otherwise it is passed through inference engine to disclose data that can be inferred. All the disclosed data obtained from inference engine is again sent to MAC to detect any direct security violation. If any violation is detected the query is rejected, otherwise answered.

13.2   References

[1] "Inference Attacks on Location Tracks" by John Krumm

[2] http://www.ics.uci.edu/~{}chenli/pub/2007-dasfaa.pdf "Protecting Individual Information Against Inference Attacks in Data Publishing" by Chen Li, Houtan Shirani-Mehr, and Xiaochun Yang

[3] "Detecting Inference Attacks Using Association Rules" by Sangeetha Raman, 2001

[4] "Database Security Issues: Inference" by Mike Chapple

Chapter 14

Java Data Mining

Java Data Mining (**JDM**) is a standard Java API for developing data mining applications and tools. JDM defines an object model and Java API for data mining objects and processes. JDM enables applications to integrate data mining technology for developing predictive analytics applications and tools. The JDM 1.0 standard was developed under the Java Community Process as JSR 73. In 2006, the JDM 2.0 specification was being developed under JSR 247, but has been withdrawn in 2011 without standardization.

Various data mining functions and techniques like statistical classification and association, regression analysis, data clustering, and attribute importance are covered by the 1.0 release of this standard.

14.1 See also

- AIDA (Abstract Interfaces for Data Analysis) is a language-neutral standard, with a Java implementation

- Mark F. Hornick, Erik Marcade, Sunil Venkayala: "Java Data Mining: Strategy, Standard, And Practice: A Practical Guide for Architecture, Design, And Implementation" (Broché)

- SCaViS Java data analysis and data mining framework that supports scripting languages

- Weka (machine learning)

- Apache Mahout

14.2 Books

- Java Data Mining: Strategy, Standard, and Practice, Hornick, Marcadé, Venkayala, ISBN 0-12-370452-9

14.3 External links

- JSR 247 (JDM 2.0)

- JSR 73 (JDM 1.0)

- Datamining (java.net project)

- Java Data Mining concepts article by Mark F. Hornick, Erik Marcadé, and Sunil Venkayala, at JavaWorld.com

- Mine Your Own Data with the JDM API article by Frank Sommers

- Using Java Data Mining to Develop Advanced Analytics Applications article by Sunil Venkayala at SYS-CON JDM Article

Chapter 15

Open-source intelligence

Open-source intelligence (**OSINT**) is intelligence collected from publicly available sources.[1] In the intelligence community (IC), the term "open" refers to overt, publicly available sources (as opposed to covert or clandestine sources); it is not related to open-source software or public intelligence.

15.1   Open sources for intelligence

OSINT includes a wide variety of information and sources:

- Media: newspapers, magazines, radio, television, and computer-based information.

- Web-based communities and user-generated content: social-networking sites, video sharing sites, wikis, blogs, and folksonomies.

- Public data: government reports, official data such as budgets, demographics, hearings, legislative debates, press conferences, speeches, marine and aeronautical safety warnings, environmental impact statements and contract awards.

- Observation and reporting: amateur airplane spotters, radio monitors and satellite observers among many others have provided significant information not otherwise available. The availability of worldwide satellite photography, often of high resolution, on the Web (e.g., Google Earth) has expanded open-source capabilities into areas formerly available only to major intelligence services.

- Professional and academic (including grey literature): conferences, symposia, professional associations, academic papers, and subject matter experts.[2]

- Most information has geospatial dimensions, but many often overlook the geospatial side of OSINT: not all open-source data is unstructured text. Examples of geospatial open source include hard and softcopy maps, atlases, gazetteers, port plans, gravity data, aeronautical data, navigation data, geodetic data, human terrain data (cultural and economic), environmental data, commercial imagery, LIDAR, hyper and multi-spectral data, airborne imagery, geo-names, geo-features, urban terrain, vertical obstruction data, boundary marker data, geospatial mashups, spatial databases, and web services. Most of the geospatial data mentioned above is integrated, analyzed, and syndicated using geospatial software like a Geographic Information System (GIS) not a browser *per se*.

OSINT is distinguished from research in that it applies the process of intelligence to create tailored knowledge supportive of a specific decision by a specific individual or group.[3]

15.2   Definers for OSINT

OSINT is defined by both the U.S. Director of National Intelligence and the U.S. Department of Defense (DoD), as "produced from publicly available information that is collected, exploited, and disseminated in a timely manner to an appropriate audience for the purpose of addressing a specific intelligence requirement."[4]

OSINT is, as of 2005, defined by the U.S. Office of Management and Budget under the category of "Forces And Direct Support" and specifically for the DoD under Commercial Code M320 as[5]

Open-source intelligence (OSINT) collection/processing

A wide variety of vendors sell information products specifically within this category.

Open-source intelligence under one name or another has been around for hundreds of years. The significance today of OSINT in the USA is the conflict between military, government, and the private sector as to how the bulk of intelligence should be obtained. With the Internet, instant communications, and advanced media search the bulk of actionable and predictive intelligence can be obtained from public, unclassified sources. Government agencies have been slow to embrace OSINT, or believe they already have suitable information feeds from the media, academia and public records.

OSINT is especially helpful in addressing global coverage, a term encompassing all of the countries and topics that are not considered by the secret or national security worlds to be "vital."

15.3   Competitive intelligence

In the private sector, competitive intelligence has become a tool for marketing strategies that focus on strategically prepared information under the direction of private companies or individuals who sell organized information to specific security, law enforcement and military industries, amongst other strategic applications, often on a contractual basis. Governments and civilians both use open source intelligence, both legitimately and illegitimately, the latter being the case with criminals who use information to gain an edge in planning and conducting criminal activities.

There are still opportunities for small and medium businesses to compete in niche markets, but this too is being consolidated by major information providers (e.g.?). OSINT is not a novel concept in media where everyday operations of traditional newsroom methods of operations engage in useful strategies towards obtaining information for unique and original content through investigations of story leads, absent of reliance on formal methods of obtaining inside information through legal documents or basic interview techniques. Investigative journalists use searches, databases, primary interviews, original sources, and leaks (informants/witnesses) who come forward either anonymously or openly, as direct contributors of inside information for journalists. Investigative journalists use specific strategies to obtain information. Sometimes informants come forward on their own to contribute original information that might not otherwise be made available, which often directly contributes to the publication of original feature stories. Such has been the case with regard to many whistle blowers in politics, government, law enforcement and also in commercial, financial and private sectors.

15.4   Risks for practitioners

Accredited journalists have some protection in asking questions, and researching for recognized media outlets. Even so they can be imprisoned, even executed, for seeking out OSINT. Private individuals illegally collecting data for a foreign military or intelligence agency is considered espionage in most countries. Of course, espionage that is not treason (i.e. betraying one's country of citizenship) has been a tool of statecraft since ancient times, is widely engaged in by nearly all countries, and is considered an honorable trade.[6] Most countries recognize this, and if their counterintelligence agencies capture a foreign spy, that spy is usually unceremoniously deported or traded back to their homeland (for other spies) after a hostile debriefing; actual execution or refusal to trade back foreign spies with non-official cover would result in consequences in bilateral relations of the gravest possible magnitude, being an extraordinarily hostile act, even if those consequences were unofficially and extrajudicially imposed.

15.5 Value

According to the Commission on the Intelligence Capabilities of the United States Regarding Weapons of Mass Destruction report submitted in March 2005, OSINT must be included in the all-source intelligence process for the following reasons (as stated in the report):

1. The ever-shifting nature of our intelligence needs compels the IC to quickly and easily understand a wide range of foreign countries and cultures. – ... today's threats are rapidly changing and geographically diffuse; it is a fact of life that an intelligence analyst may be forced to shift rapidly from one topic to the next. Increasingly, IC professionals need to quickly assimilate social, economic, and cultural information about a country—information often detailed in open sources.

2. Open-source information provides a base for understanding classified materials. Despite large quantities of classified material produced by the IC, the amount of classified information produced on any one topic can be quite limited, and may be taken out of context if viewed only from a classified-source perspective. Perhaps the most important example today relates to terrorism, where open-source information can fill gaps and create links that allow analysts to better understand fragmented intelligence, rumored terrorist plans, possible means of attack, and potential targets.

3. Open-source materials can protect sources and methods. Sometimes an intelligence judgment that is actually informed with sensitive, classified information can be defended on the basis of open-source reporting. This can prove useful when policy-makers need to explain policy decisions or communicate with foreign officials without compromising classified sources.

4. Only open source can *store history*. A robust open-source program can, in effect, gather data to monitor the world's cultures and how they change with time. This is difficult, if not impossible, using the *snapshots* provided by classified collection methods.[7]

15.6 Process

See also: Big Data

Information collection in OSINT is generally a different problem from collection in other intelligence disciplines where obtaining the raw information to be analyzed may be the major difficulty, particularly if it is to be obtained from non-cooperative targets. In OSINT, the chief difficulty is in identifying relevant, reliable sources from the vast amount of publicly available information. However, this is not as great a challenge for those who know how to access local knowledge and how to leverage human experts who can create new tailored knowledge on the fly.

15.7 History

The Foreign Broadcast Information Service (FBIS) was created in 1941 to access and exploit OSINT in relation to World War II. A classic example of their value and success is reflected in the price of oranges in Paris as an indicator of whether railroad bridges had been bombed successfully.

The recent history of OSINT began in 1988 when General Alfred M. Gray, Jr., Commandant of the Marine Corps, called for a redirection of US intelligence away from the collapsing Soviet Union and toward non-state actors and Third World zones of instability. Additionally, he pointed out that most of the intelligence which needs to be known could be obtained via OSINT, and recommended a substantive increase in resources for this aspect of the intelligence collection spectrum of sources.[8]

In the fall of 1992, Senator David Boren, then Chairman of the Senate Select Committee on Intelligence, sponsored the National Security Act of 1992, attempting to achieve modest reform in the U.S. Intelligence Community. His counterpart on the House Permanent Select Committee on Intelligence was Congressman Dave McCurdy. The House version of the legislation included a separate open-source office, at the suggestion of Larry Prior, a Marine Reservist familiar with the MCIC experience and then serving on the House Permanent Select Committee on Intelligence staff.

The Aspin-Brown Commission stated in 1996 that US access to open sources was "severely deficient" and that this should be a "top priority" for both funding and DCI attention.

In issuing its July 2004 report, the 9/11 Commission recommended the creation of an open-source intelligence agency, but without further detail or comment.[9] Subsequently, the WMD Commission (also known as the Robb–Silberman Commission) report in March 2005 recommended the creation of an open-source directorate at the CIA.

Following these recommendations, in November 2005 the Director of National Intelligence announced the creation of the DNI Open Source Center. The Center was established to collect information available from "the Internet, databases, press, radio, television, video, geospatial data, photos and commercial imagery."[10] In addition to collecting openly available information, it would train analysts to make better use of this information. The Center absorbed the CIA's previously existing Foreign Broadcast Information Service (FBIS), originally established in 1941, with FBIS head Douglas Naquin named as director of the Center.[11]

In December 2005, the Director of National Intelligence appointed Eliot A. Jardines as the Assistant Deputy Director of National Intelligence for Open Source to serve as the Intelligence Community's senior intelligence officer for open source and to provide strategy, guidance and oversight for the National Open Source Enterprise.[12] Mr. Jardines has established the National Open Source Enterprise[13] and authored Intelligence Community Directive 301. In 2008, Mr. Jardines returned to the private sector and was succeeded by Dan Butler who is ADDNI/OS[14] and previously Mr. Jardines' Senior Advisor for Policy.[15]

15.8   OSINT communities

15.8.1   Government

There are a large number of open-source activities taking place throughout the US Government. Frequently, these open-source activities are described as "media monitoring", "media analysis", "internet research" and "public surveys" but are open source nonetheless.

The Library of Congress sponsors the Federal Research Division (FRD) which conducts a great deal of tailored open-source research on a fee-for-service basis for the executive branch.

15.8.2   Intelligence

The US Intelligence Community's open-source activities (known as the National Open Source Enterprise) are dictated by Intelligence Community Directive 301 promulgated by the Director of National Intelligence.[16] The Directive establishes the authorities and responsibilities of the Assistant Deputy Director of National Intelligence for Open Source (ADDNI/OS), the DNI's Open Source Center and the National Open Source Committee.

Prior to the establishment of the National Open Source Enterprise, the Foreign Broadcast Information Service (FBIS), established in 1941, was the government's primary open-source unit, transcribing and translating foreign broadcasts. It absorbed the Defense Department's Joint Publications Research Service (JPRS), which did a similar function with foreign printed materials, including newspapers, magazines, and technical journals.

15.8.3   Armed Forces

The former Under-Secretary of Defense for Intelligence, Dr. Stephen Cambone encouraged in part by the Defense Science Board reports on Strategic Communication and Transition to and From Hostilities, created the Defense Open Source Program (DOSP). The current Under-Secretary of Defense for Intelligence is assigned executive agency for this program to the Defense Intelligence Agency.

U.S. military offices that engage in OSINT activities include:

- Defense Intelligence Agency

- National Geospatial-Intelligence Agency

- US Army Foreign Military Studies Office

- US Army Asian Studies Detachment

- EUCOM JAC Molesworth

- Foreign Media Monitoring in Support of Information Operations, U.S. Strategic Command

15.8.4 Homeland Security

The Department of Homeland Security has an active open-source intelligence unit. In congressional testimony before the House Homeland Security Committee's Intelligence, Information Sharing and Terrorism Risk Assessment Subcommittee the Undersecretary of Homeland Security Charles Allen indicated on February 14, 2007, that he had established the "Domestic Open Source Enterprise" to support the Department's OSINT needs and that of state, local and tribal partners.

15.8.5 Law enforcement

The law enforcement OSINT community applies open-source intelligence (OSINT) to the prediction, prevention, investigation, and prosecution of criminals including terrorists.

Examples of successful law enforcement OSINT include Scotland Yard OSINT; Royal Canadian Mounted Police (RCMP) OSINT.

INTERPOL and EUROPOL experimented with OSINT units for a time, but they appear to have atrophied with the departure of their individual champions.

New York Police Department (NYPD) is known to have an OSINT unit, as does the Los Angeles County Sheriff's Department, housed within the Emergency Operations Bureau and affiliated with the LA Joint Regional Intelligence Center.

15.8.6 Business

Business OSINT encompasses Commercial Intelligence, Competitor Intelligence, and Business Intelligence, and is often a chief area of practice of private intelligence agencies.

Businesses may use information brokers and private investigators to collect and analyze relevant information for business purposes which may include the media, deep web, web 2.0 and commercial content.

15.9   See also

- Wikipedia

- Intellipedia

- Open Source Center

- Private intelligence agency

- ROSIDS

- Special Libraries Association

- Strategic intelligence

- NATO Open Source Intelligence Handbook, NATO Open Source Intelligence Reader

- MiTAP

- DARPA TIDES program

- Investigative Data Warehouse

- Fusion Center

- National Intelligence Open Source Committee

15.10   References

[1] "Open Source Intelligence" (PDF).

[2] Lowenthal, Mark M. *Intelligence: From Secrets to Policy*, 2nd Ed. (Washington, D.C.: CQ Press, 2003) p. 79.

[3] "Spy Agencies Turn to Newspapers, NPR, and Wikipedia for Information: The intelligence community is learning to value 'open-source' information". Retrieved 2008-09-15.

[4] As defined in Sec. 931 of Public Law 109-163, entitled, "National Defense Authorization Act for Fiscal Year 2006."

[5] FAIR Act Inventory Commercial Activities Inventory Function Codes

[6] Sun Tzu (Warring States period), *The Art of War*, Chapter 13: "Hostile armies may face each other for years, striving for the victory which is decided in a single day. This being so, to remain in ignorance of the enemy's condition simply because one grudges the outlay of a hundred ounces of silver in honors and emoluments, is the height of inhumanity."

[7] (The Commission on the Intelligence Capabilities, 378–379). Commission on the Intelligence Capabilities of the United States Regarding Weapons of Mass Destruction

[8] General Alfred M. Gray, "Global Intelligence Challenges in the 1990s", American Intelligence Journal (Winter 1989–1990)

[9] See page 413 of the 9-11 Commission Report (pdf).

[10] Office of the Director of National Intelligence. "ODNI Announces Establishment of Open Source Center". Press release, 8 November 2005.

[11] Ensor, David. "The Situation Report: Open source intelligence center". *CNN*, 8 November 2005.

[12] Office of the Director of National Intelligence "ODNI Senior Leadership Announcement". Press release, 7 December 2005.

[13] "National Open Source Entreprise Vision Statement" May 2006

[14] DNI Open Source Conference 2008 "Decision Advantage" agenda, Office of the Director of National Intelligence, July 2008.

[15] DNI Open Source Conference 2007 "Expanding the Horizons" agenda, Office of the Director of National Intelligence, July 2007.

[16] DNI Intelligence Community Directive 301 – "National Open Source Enterprise" 11 July 2006.

- WashTimes.com, Washington Times – CIA mines 'rich' content from blogs, 19 April 2006

- GCN.com, Government Computer News – Intelligence units mine the benefits of public sources 20 March 2006

- AFCEA.org, SIGNAL Magazine – Intelligence Center Mines Open Sources March 2006

- FindAcricles.com, Military Intelligence Professional Bulletin October–December, 2005 by Barbara G. Fast

- FAS.org, Congressional Testimony on OSINT and Homeland Security 21 June 2005

- FirstMonday.org, Open Source Intelligence by Stalder and Hirsh, 15 May 2002

- Forbes.com, When Everyone Can Mine Your Data by Taylor Buley, 11.21.08]

- , Open-Source Spying, article from the *New York Times*, about open sources and wikis

- Cnet.com, Maltego and the science of 'open-source' snooping by Matt Asay, November 25, 2008

15.11 Literature

Scientific Publications

- Arthuer S. Hulnick: 'The Dilemma of Open Source Intelligence: Is OSINT Really Intelligence?', pages 229–241, The Oxford Handbook of National Security Intelligence, 2010

- Cody Burke: 'Freeing knowledge, telling secrets: Open source intelligence and development', Bond University, May 2007

- Florian Schaurer, Jan Störger: 'The Evolution of Open Source Intelligence', OSINT Report 3/2010, ISN, ETH Zürich, October 2010

- Mikel Rufián: "OSINT Training Workshop": OSINT Analyst: Advance Techniques, Tools and Training', Spain 2010

15.12 External links

General

- An OSINT Deep Web Search for usersnames and email addresses

- The Open Source Intelligence Resource Discovery Toolkit

- The New Craft of Intelligence: Making the Most of Open Private Sector Knowledge

- Actual Intelligence Case Studies Leveraging Open Source Intelligence (OSINT)

- Sailing the Sea of OSINT in the Information Age

- The Intelligence Network

- OSINT discussion group at Yahoo!

- Open Source Center – U.S. government arm focusing on open source intelligence under the DNI

- The OSINT Catalogue of reports and books

- Collection and Use of Open-Source Intelligence – A to Z

- Open Source Intelligence (OSINT): Issues for Congress, Congressional Research Service, December 5, 2007

- Open Source Intelligence (OSINT): Issues for Congress, Congressional Research Service, January 28, 2008

Advocacy and analysis of OSINT

- FindArticles.com, FMSO-JRIC and Open Source Intelligence: speaking prose in a world of verse, Military Intelligence Professional Bulletin, Oct–Dec, 2005 by Jacob W. Kipp

Information Security

- The collective intelligence framework

Chapter 16

Path analysis (computing)

Path analysis, is the analysis of a path, which is a portrayal of a chain of consecutive events that a given user or cohort performs during a set period of time while using a website, online game, or eCommerce platform. As a subset of behavioral analytics, path analysis is a way to understand user behavior in order to gain actionable insights into the data. Path analysis provides a visual portrayal of every event a user or cohort performs as part of a path during a set period of time.

While it is possible to track a user's path through the site, and even show that path as a visual representation, the real question is how to gain these actionable insights. If path analysis simply outputs a "pretty"[1] graph, while it may look nice, it does not provide anything concrete to act upon.

16.1 Examples

In order to get the most out of path analysis the first step would be to determine what needs to be analyzed and what are the goals of the analysis. A company might be trying to figure out why their site is running slow, are certain types of users interested in certain pages or products, or if their user interface is set up in a logical way.

Now that the goal has been set there are a few ways of performing the analysis. If a large percentage of a certain cohort, people between the ages of 18-25, logs into an online game, creates a profile and then spends the next 10 minutes wandering around the menu page, then it may be that the user interface is not logical. By seeing this group of users following the path that they did a developer will be able to analyze the data and realize that after creating a profile, the "play game" button does not appear. Thus, path analysis was able to provide actionable data for the company to act on and fix an error.

In eCommerce, path analysis can help customize a shopping experience to each user. By looking at what products other customers in a certain cohort looked at before buying one, a company can suggest "items you may also like" to the next customer and increase the chances of them making a purchase. Also, path analysis can help solve performance issues on a platform. For example, a company looks at a path and realizes that their site freezes up after a certain combinations of events. By analyzing the path and the progression of events that led to the error, the company can pinpoint the error and fix it.

16.2 Evolution

Historically path analysis fell under the broad category of website analytics, and related only to the analysis of paths through websites. Path analysis in website analytics is a process of determining a sequence of pages visited in a visitor session prior to some desired event, such as the visitor purchasing an item or requesting a newsletter. The precise order of pages visited may or may not be important and may or may not be specified. In practice, this analysis is done in aggregate, ranking the paths (sequences of pages) visited prior to the desired event, by descending frequency of use. The idea is to determine what features of the website encourage the desired result. "Fallout analysis," a subset of path analysis, looks at "black holes" on the site, or paths that lead to a dead end most frequently, paths or features that confuse or lose potential customers. [2]

With the advent of big data along with web based applications, online games, and eCommerce platforms, path analysis has come to include much more than just web path analysis. Understanding how users move through an app, game, or other web platform are all part of modern day path analysis.

16.3 Understanding visitors

In the real world when you visit a shop the shelves and products are not placed in a random order. The shop owner carefully analyzes the visitors and path they walk through the shop, especially when they are selecting or buying products. Next the shop owner will reorder the shelves and products to optimize sales by putting everything in the most logical order for the visitors. In a supermarket this will typically result in the wine shelf next to a variety of cookies, chips, nuts, etc. Simply because people drink wine and eat nuts with it.

In most web sites there is a same logic that can be applied. Visitors who have questions about a product will go to the product information or support section of a web site. From there they make a logical step to the frequently asked questions page if they have a specific question. A web site owner also wants to analyze visitor behavior. For example if a web site offers products for sale, the owner wants to convert as many visitors to a completed purchase. If there is a sign-up form with multiple pages, web site owners want to guide visitors to the final sign-up page.

Path analysis answers typical questions like:
Where do most visitors go after they enter my home page?
Is there a strong visitor relation between product A and product B on my web site?.
Questions that can't be answered by page hits and unique visitors statistics.

16.4 Funnels and goals

Google Analytics provides a path function with funnels and goals. A predetermined path of web site pages is specified and every visitor walking the path is a goal. This approach is very helpful when analyzing how many visitors reach a certain destination page, called an end point analysis.[3]

16.5 Using maps

The paths visitors walk in a web site can lead to an endless number of unique paths. As a result there is no point in analyzing each path, but to look for the strongest paths. These strongest paths are typically shown in a graphical map or in text like: Page A --> Page B --> Page D --> Exit.

16.6 See also

- Funnel analysis

- Cohort analysis

- website analytics

- Big data

- Data mining

- Analytics

- Business Intelligence
- Test and Learn
- Business Process Discovery
- Statistics
- Customer dynamics
- Behavioral analytics

16.7 References

[1] Thayer, Shelby. "Why Do We Care About Path Analysis?". *Trending Upward.*

[2] "Path analysis (computing) [archived]". Wikipedia User: Lgallindo.

[3] "Analysis Tools". Google Analytics.

16.8 Further reading

- "Determining Visitor Behavior Patterns". *Web Analytics Tutorial.*
- Gupta, Srishti. "Is User Path Analysis The Right Path?".
- Harris, Jeff. "Big Data and Predictive Analytics" (PDF). Xerox Services.
- Cutroni, Justin. "Path Analysis in Google Analytics with Flow Visualization". *Analytics Talk.*
- "Big Data" (PDF). *Technology Roadmap.* Infocomm Development Authority of Sinagapore.
- Coren, Yehoshua. "Understanding Google Analytics Multi Channel Funnels". Online-Behavior.com.

Chapter 17

Police-enforced ANPR in the UK

Closed-circuit television cameras such as these can be used to take the images scanned by automatic number plate recognition systems

The UK has an extensive automatic number plate recognition (ANPR) CCTV network. Police and security services use it to track UK vehicle movements in real time. The resulting data are stored for 2 years in the National ANPR Data Centre to be analyzed for intelligence and to be used as evidence.[1]

Following the formation of the Conservative – Liberal Democrat Coalition after the 2010 General Election, it was announced in July 2010 that the system is to be placed under statutory regulation. This is likely to establish a right in law to collect the data, and place controls on its use, storage and access by third parties.[2] The Protection of Freedoms Act 2012 was enacted in order to provide for tighter regulation of ANPR.

17.1 The ANPR CCTV network

The London congestion charge scheme uses two hundred and thirty cameras and ANPR to help monitor vehicles in the charging zone

Since March 2006, most motorways, main roads, town centres, London's congestion charge zone,[3] ports and petrol station forecourts have been covered by CCTV camera networks using automatic number plate recognition. Existing traffic cameras in towns and cities are being converted to read number plates automatically as part of the new national surveillance network.

> "What we're trying to do as far as we can is to stitch together the existing camera network rather than install a huge number of new cameras," - Mr Whiteley chairman of the ANPR steering committee said.[1]

Some cameras may be disguised for covert operations but the majority will be ordinary CCTV traffic cameras converted to read number plates.[1] Every police force will also have a fleet of specially fitted police vans with ANPR cameras.[1] All data generated is fed to The National ANPR Data Centre.

One camera can cover many motorway lanes. Just two ANPR devices, for instance, cover north and south movements through the 27 lanes of the Dartford crossing toll area on the Thames. Whiteley said the intention eventually was to move from the "low thousands" of cameras to the "high thousands".[1]

17.2 National ANPR Data Centre

The National ANPR Data Centre stores all ANPR data feed from the various police forces, currently it does not take data from CCTV networks in the UK.[4] The National ANPR Data Centre is based at Hendon in north London, the site of the existing Police National Computer. In March 2006 the National ANPR Data Centre could store 50 million number plate 'reads' per day,[5] to be expanded to 100 million 'reads' per day within a couple of years. The time, date and place of each vehicle sighting will be stored for two years.[1] At the present 27 million clocks a day, over 18 billion ANPR records would be recorded every year. According to the National Policing Improvement Agency 25,000 hits per day against the ANPR database generate a transaction against the Police National Computer.[6]

17.2.1 Crosschecks

CCTV cameras

The National ANPR Data Centre is being built alongside the Police National Computer because of the need to be constantly updated with lists of suspect drivers and vehicles.[1] Car registrations are checked against lists from the Police National Computer, including vehicles of interest to the police for crimes such as burglary or theft of petrol. Uninsured drivers will be identified from data provided by the insurance industry, vehicles without a valid MoT test certificate will be flagged, and vehicles without a valid tax disc or with unlawful number plates will be identified.

The National ANPR Data Centre allows analysis across police force boundaries.[4] If a vehicle enters the ANPR network, the police should have an image of it entering the area, which may also show the driver and passenger. As the data generated is stored for two years the police argue criminals could be identified and linked to vehicles.[4]

17.2.2 Data mining

A major feature of the National ANPR Data Centre for car numbers is the ability to data mine. Advanced versatile automated data mining software trawls through the vast amounts of data collected, finding patterns and meaning in the data. Data mining can be used on the records of previous sightings to build up intelligence of a vehicle's movements on the road network or can be used to find cloned vehicles by searching the database for impossibly quick journeys.[1][4]

> "We can use ANPR on investigations or we can use it looking forward in a proactive, intelligence way. Things like building up the lifestyle of criminals - where they are going to be at certain times. We seek to link the criminal to the vehicle through intelligence. Vehicles moving on the roads are open to police scrutiny at any time. The Road Traffic Act gives us the right to stop vehicles at any time for any purpose" - Frank Whiteley, Chief Constable of Hertfordshire and Chair of the ACPO ANPR Steering Group[1]

17.2.3 The database

The National ANPR Data Centre uses an Oracle database, and custom-written Java software with specific police networks rather than the internet used to send and receive data.[4] The design of the system will also take into account future changes to the way cars will be recognised, such as electronic vehicle identification - when a unique identity chip is built into the bodywork.[1]

17.3 Data access

17.3.1 Police

The police have real-time access to all ANPR camera data. Effectively, the police (and the security services) can track any car (technically any numberplate) around the country in close to real time.[3]

Every police force will have direct computer access to the National ANPR Data Centre. The current restraints on police use of ANPR data have been dictated by pragmatism rather than a concern for civil liberties. Giving every police officer free access to the system would overload the system, "make it unstable, slow it down", said John Dean, National ANPR co-ordinator for the Association of Chief Police Officers.[5] ANPR records younger than 91 days can only be accessed on the NADC with an Inspector's authority to investigate serious and major crime. Enquiries over 90 days to a year require a Superintendent's authority and any searches over a year require a Superintendent's authority and must be for Counter Terrorism only.

Mobile ANPR systems such as ProVida ANPR are becoming more popular, with forces having systems in traffic police intercept cars. The advantage of this is that officers can get real time 'hits' from passing vehicles as they are on patrol.

17.4 ANPR cases

17.4.1   Positive use

In August 2004 a presentation by John Dean, the Association of Chief Police Officers' (ACPO) National ANPR Co-ordinator at IFSEC revealed how ANPR was being used to 'deny criminals the use of the road'.[7]

On 18 November 2005 British police constable Sharon Beshenivsky was shot and killed during a robbery in Bradford. The CCTV network was linked into an ANPR system and was able to identify the getaway car and track its movements, leading to the arrest of six suspects. At its launch in May, Ch Supt Geoff Dodd of West Yorkshire Police, called the ANPR system a "revolutionary tool in detecting crime".[8]

17.4.2   Car cloning

The success of ANPR in detecting vehicles of interest to police has led to a new kind of crime - car cloning. Criminals target vehicles of the same make and model to copy these number plates so that ANPR systems will record a read on the make and model relating to a fake number plate. Any legal transgressions could then lead to the legitimate owner receiving notification of enforcement action instead of the criminal. There is very little monitoring of number plate manufacture, particularly websites offering "vanity plates" (plates that are usable only in off-road circumstances, such as car shows) and this gives criminals avenues to attempt to evade detection, however ANPR will often show that there are multiple vehicles using the same registration number and prove that the genuine owner is innocent as well as providing images to identify the culprits.[9]

17.4.3   Project Champion

Project Champion is a project to install a £3m network of 169 ANPR cameras to monitor vehicles entering and leaving the Sparkbrook and Washwood Heath neighbourhoods of Birmingham, both of which have large Muslim communities. Its implementation was frozen in June 2010 amid allegations that the police deliberately misled councillors about its purpose, after it was revealed that it was being funded as an anti-terrorism initiative, rather than for 'reassurance and crime prevention'.[10][11]

17.5   History

17.5.1   Project Laser in the United Kingdom

In March 2005, plans were announced to set up a nationwide system of over 2,000 automatic number plate recognition cameras in the United Kingdom.

This followed the successful rollout of Project Spectrum in which all 43 Police Forces in England and Wales were supplied by the Home Office with an ANPR capable mobile unit, and a 'Back Office'. A subsequent series of trials were then commenced in 2002 when the Vehicle and Operator Services Agency (VOSA) was given funding by the Home Office to work with the Police Standards Unit and develop "**Project Laser**" using the equipment supplied under Project Spectrum. With the aim of running the ANPR system nationwide, it was initially trialled by nine police forces and ran between 30 September 2002 and March 2003. Those police forces covered the areas of Greater Manchester, North Wales, Avon and Somerset, Northampton, London, Kent, West Yorkshire, Staffordshire and West Midlands

The second phase of the project ran between 1 June 2003 and 21 June 2004 and involved 23 police forces in total. The DVLA is also involved with Project Laser, using the system to gather details on unregistered and unlicensed vehicles and those without a valid MOT certificate or insurance cover.

> "Eventually the database will link to most CCTV systems in town centres, meaning that all vehicles filmed on one of the many cameras protecting Bedford High Street, for instance, can be checked against the database and the movements of wanted cars traced to help with serious crime investigations."
> — Bedfordshire Police

The project was seen as a success despite a Home Office report showing that the Driver and Vehicle Licensing Agency (DVLA) trial had an error rate of up to 40%, with claims that the system was contributing

"...in excess of 100 arrests per officer per year – ten times the national average..."[12]

Further findings went on to show that the error rate dropped to 5% when infrared systems and more regular updates of information were used.

During the second phase of the project around 28 million number plates were spotted in total, with 1.1 million (3.9%) of these matching an entry in one of the databases. 180,543 vehicles were stopped (101,775 directly because of the ANPR system), leading to 13,499 arrests (7.5% of the total) and the issue of 50,910 fines (28.2%). 1,152 stolen vehicles (worth £7.5 million in total), £380,000 worth of drugs and £640,000 worth of stolen goods were also recovered. The primary goal of the second phase was to see how well the costs of the ANPR system could be covered. The final conclusion was that less than 10% of the expenditure incurred was recouped, with the Home Office claiming that the failure of drivers to pay fines contributed to this low figure, and continued to recommend the system be deployed throughout the UK. Report (PDF)

Funding is now in place for the construction of the National ANPR Data Centre capable of holding 50 million ANPR reads per day, destined to form the basis of a vehicle movement database.[13]

There have been sensationalist stories in the national press suggesting that the use of the network could be extended to catch drivers using mobile phones illegally, and those failing to wear seat belts.[14] The current system only retains text-strings consisting of number, date, & time. Saving images would require a huge increase in both transmission-speed and storage-space (along with image-recognition software to detect phone and/or seat-belts at motorway traffic speeds).

17.6   Criticism

Speaking on 14 September 2008, Simon Davies, the director of Privacy International stated that the database would give police "extraordinary powers of surveillance" and claimed that "this would never be allowed in any other democratic country".[15]

John Catt, an 80-year-old pensioner at the time and his daughter Linda (with no criminal record between them) - were stopped on 31 July 2005, had their vehicle searched under section 44 of the Terrorism Act 2000 by City of London Police and were threatened with arrest if they refused to answer police questions. After making formal police complaints, it was discovered they were stopped after their vehicle had been picked up by roadside ANPR CCTV cameras, after a marker had been placed against their vehicle in the Police National Computer database as a result of them being spotted attending EDO MBM demonstrations in Brighton. Supporters of the Catts highlight the fact that John and Linda Catt had been suspected of no crime, and argue that they were unfairly targeted due to their associations.[16] Police spokesmen described the campaign Catt had been taking part in as a "campaign of illegality designed to pressurise EDO to cease its lawful business" which led to a series of convictions of campaigners, and argued that surveillance of Catt was necessary because "his voluntary association at the Smash EDO protests forms part of a far wider picture of information which it is necessary for the police to continue to monitor in order to plan to maintain the peace, minimise the risks of criminal offending and adequately to detect and prosecute offenders".[17] Sussex Police refused to confirm or deny whether a tag exists on their car. As of February 2012 John Catt did not have a criminal record. Catt commented "That our participation in peaceful protest outside an arms factory led to our arbitrary stop-check for terrorist activities many miles away by another force is a very disturbing development of the 'police state'."[18]

The Register has noted that "in theory a system could be organised in such a way that records of law-abiding drivers weren't generated at all, but that hasn't been the way things have panned out."[19]

17.7   See also

- Civil liberties in the United Kingdom

- Mass surveillance in the United Kingdom

- Privacy

17.8   References

[1] Connor, Steve (22 December 2005). "Surveillance UK: why this revolution is only the start". *The Independent* (London). Retrieved 20 September 2007.

[2] 'Big brother' traffic cameras must be regulated, orders home secretary, The Guardian, published 2010-07-04. Retrieved 14 August 2010

[3] "Met given real time c-charge data". *BBC.* 17 July 2007. Retrieved 20 September 2007.

[4] Mathieson, SA (15 February 2007). "http://society.guardian.co.uk/e-public/story/0,,2012997,00.html". *the Guardian* (London). Retrieved 20 September 2007.

[5] "UK car tracking database delayed to boost capacity". *the Register.* Retrieved 20 September 2007.

[6] National Policing Improvement Agency Business Plan 2009-10. Page 32.

[7] http://www.securitysa.com/article.aspx?pklArticleId=3093&pklCategoryId=22

[8] "CCTV network tracks 'getaway' car" at BBC News, 21 November 2005

[9] "Inside Car Cloning" at BBC Inside Out, 3 December 2009

[10] Police under fire over Muslim CCTV surveillance scheme, The Guardian, published 2010-06-18. Retrieved 14 August 2010

[11] Birmingham stops Muslim CCTV surveillance scheme, The Guardian, 2010-06-17. Retrieved 14 August 2010

[12] "Automatic Number Plate Recognition (ANPR)". Police Standards Unit, PoliceReform.gov.uk.

[13] UK car tracking database delayed to boost capacity 18 April 2006

[14] Surveillance on drivers may be increased 7 March 2006

[15] Fears over privacy as police expand surveillance project The Guardian, 2008-09-15. Retrieved 15 September 2008

[16] Watching You, SchNEWS 625, 20 March 2008

[17] Protester sues police over surveillance database, *The Guardian*

[18] Brighton Argus: Brighton pensioner slams "police state" after terror police tag car

[19] UK.gov plans more active-traffic motorway ANPR cams The Register, 2007-10-26. Retrieved 8 June 2009

Chapter 18

Proactive Discovery of Insider Threats Using Graph Analysis and Learning

Proactive Discovery of Insider Threats Using Graph Analysis and Learning or **PRODIGAL** is a computer system for predicting anomalous behavior amongst humans by data mining network traffic such as emails, text messages and log entries.[1] It is part of DARPA's Anomaly Detection at Multiple Scales (ADAMS) project.[2] The initial schedule is for two years and the budget $9 million.[3]

It uses graph theory, machine learning, statistical anomaly detection, and high-performance computing to scan larger sets of data more quickly than in past systems. The amount of data analyzed is in the range of terabytes per day.[3] The targets of the analysis are employees within the government or defense contracting organizations; specific examples of behavior the system is intended to detect include the actions of Nidal Malik Hasan and Wikileaks alleged source Chelsea Manning.[1] Commercial applications may include finance.[1] The results of the analysis, the five most serious threats per day, go to agents, analysts, and operators working in counterintelligence.[1][3][4]

18.1   Primary participants

- Georgia Institute of Technology College of Computing

- Georgia Tech Research Institute

- Defense Advanced Research Projects Agency

- Army Research Office

- Science Applications International Corporation

- Oregon State University

- University of Massachusetts Amherst

- Carnegie Mellon University

18.2   See also

- Cyber Insider Threat

- Einstein (US-CERT program)

- Threat (computer)

- Intrusion detection

- Echelon, Thinthread, Trailblazer, Turbulence (NSA programs)

- Fusion center, Investigative Data Warehouse (FBI)

18.3   References

[1] "Video Interview: DARPA's ADAMS Project Taps Big Data to Find the Breaking Bad". Inside HPC. 2011-11-29. Retrieved 2011-12-05.

[2] Brandon, John (2011-12-03). "Could the U.S. Government Start Reading Your Emails?". Fox News. Retrieved 2011-12-06.

[3] "Georgia Tech Helps to Develop System That Will Detect Insider Threats from Massive Data Sets". Georgia Institute of Technology. 2011-11-10. Retrieved 2011-12-06.

[4] Storm, Darlene (2011-12-06). "Sifting through petabytes: PRODIGAL monitoring for lone wolf insider threats". *Computer World*. Retrieved 2011-12-06.

Chapter 19

SEMMA

SEMMA is an acronym that stands for *Sample*, *Explore*, *Modify*, *Model* and *Assess*. It is a list of sequential steps developed by SAS Institute Inc., one of the largest producers of statistics and business intelligence software. It guides the implementation of data mining applications.[1] Although SEMMA is often considered to be a general data mining methodology, SAS claims that it is "rather a logical organisation of the functional tool set of" one of their products, SAS Enterprise Miner, "for carrying out the core tasks of data mining".[2]

19.1   Background

In the expanding field of data mining, there has been a call for a standard methodology or a simply list of best practices for the diversified and iterative process of data mining that users can apply to their data mining projects regardless of industry. While the Cross Industry Standard Process for Data Mining or CRISP-DM, founded by the European Strategic Program on Research in Information Technology initiative, aimed to create a neutral methodology, SAS also offered a pattern to follow in its data mining tools.

19.2   Phases of SEMMA

The phases of SEMMA and related tasks are the following:[2]

- **Sample**. The process starts with data sampling, e.g., selecting the data set for modeling. The data set should be large enough to contain sufficient information to retrieve, yet small enough to be used efficiently. This phase also deals with data partitioning.

- **Explore**. This phase covers the understanding of the data by discovering anticipated and unanticipated relationships between the variables, and also abnormalities, with the help of data visualization.

- **Modify**. The Modify phase contains methods to select, create and transform variables in preparation for data modeling.

- **Model**. In the Model phase the focus is on applying various modeling (data mining) techniques on the prepared variables in order to create models that possibly provide the desired outcome.

- **Assess**. The last phase is Assess. The evaluation of the modeling results shows the reliability and usefulness of the created models.

19.3   Criticism

SEMMA mainly focuses on the modeling tasks of data mining projects, leaving the business aspects out (unlike, i.e., CRISP-DM and its Business Understanding phase). Additionally, SEMMA is designed to help the users of the SAS Enterprise Miner software. Therefore, applying it outside Enterprise Miner can be ambiguous.[3]

19.4   See also

- Cross Industry Standard Process for Data Mining

19.5   References

[1] Azevedo, A. and Santos, M. F. KDD, SEMMA and CRISP-DM: a parallel overview. In Proceedings of the IADIS European Conference on Data Mining 2008, pp 182-185.

[2] SAS Enterprise Miner website

[3] Rohanizadeh, S. S. and Moghadam, M. B. A Proposed Data Mining Methodology and its Application to Industrial Procedures Journal of Industrial Engineering **4** (2009) pp 37-50.

Chapter 20

Stellar Wind

For flows of particles from stars, see stellar wind.

Stellar Wind or **Stellarwind** is the code name of information collected under the President's Surveillance Program (PSP).[1] The National Security Agency (NSA) program was approved by President George W. Bush shortly after the September 11, 2001 attacks and was revealed by Thomas Tamm to *The New York Times* in 2008.[2][3] Stellar Wind was a prelude to new legal structures that allowed President Bush and President Barack Obama to reproduce each of those programs and expand their reach.[4]

20.1   Scope of the program

The program's activities involved data mining of a large database of the communications of American citizens, including e-mail communications, telephone conversations, financial transactions, and Internet activity.[3] William Binney, a retired technical leader with the NSA, discussed some of the architectural and operational elements of the program at the 2012 Chaos Communication Congress.[5]

The intelligence community also was able to obtain from the U.S. Treasury Department suspicious activity reports, or "SARS", which are reports of activities such as large cash transactions that are submitted by financial institutions under anti-money laundering rules.[3]

There were internal disputes within the U.S. Justice Department about the legality of the program, because data are collected for large numbers of people, not just the subjects of Foreign Intelligence Surveillance Act (FISA) warrants.[5][6] During the Bush Administration, the Stellarwind cases were referred to by FBI agents as "pizza cases" because many seemingly suspicious cases turned out to be food takeout orders. According to then-FBI Director Robert Mueller, approximately 99% of the cases led nowhere, but "it's that other 1% that we've got to be concerned about".[2]

20.2   2004 conflict

From a report by the inspectors general of six US intelligence agencies that was declassified in September 2015, it became clear that president Bush had originally authorized the collection of telephone and e-mail metadata only if one end of the communications was foreign or when there was a link to terrorism. But in 2004, the Justice Department found out that the NSA was apperently also collecting the metadata of purely domestic communications, after which president Bush declared that NSA had always been allowed to do so, but that analysts were only allowed to look at metadata related to terrorism. With this revised formulation, Bush reauthorized the program on March 11, 2004.[7]

In 2004, the head of the Office of Legal Counsel, Jack Landman Goldsmith, wrote at least two legal memos authorizing the program, "We conclude only that when the nation has been thrust into an armed conflict by a foreign attack on the

United States and the president determines in his role as commander in chief . . . that it is essential for defense against a further foreign attack to use the [wiretapping] capabilities of the [National Security Agency] within the United States, he has inherent constitutional authority" to order warrantless wiretapping — "an authority that Congress cannot curtail," Goldsmith wrote in a 108-page memo dated May 6, 2004. In March 2004, the OLC concluded the e-mail program was not legal, and then-Acting Attorney General James Comey refused to reauthorize it.[8]

20.3   Revelations

In March 2012 *Wired* magazine published "The NSA Is Building the Country's Biggest Spy Center (Watch What You Say)" talking about a vast new NSA facility in Utah and said, "For the first time, a former NSA official has gone on the record to describe the program, codenamed Stellarwind, in detail," naming the official William Binney, a former NSA code breaker. Binney went on to say that the NSA had highly secured rooms that tap into major switches, and satellite communications at both AT&T and Verizon.[9] The article suggested that the supposedly-dispatched Stellarwind continues as an active program. This conclusion was supported by the exposure of Room 641A in AT&T's operations center in San Francisco in 2006.

In June 2013 the *Washington Post* and the *Guardian* published an OIG draft report, dated March 2009, leaked by Edward Snowden detailing the Stellarwind program.[1][10] No doubt remained about the continuing nature of the surveillance program.

In September 2014 *The New York Times* asserted, "Questions persist after the release of a newly declassified version of a legal memo approving the National Security Agency's Stellarwind program, a set of warrantless surveillance and data collection activities secretly authorized after the terrorist attacks of Sept. 11, 2001." as an introductory headline summary with a link. The accompanying article addressed the release of a newly declassified version of the May 2004 memo.[11] Note was made that the bulk of the program, the telephone, Internet, and e-mail surveillance of American citizens, remained secret until the revelations by Edward Snowden and that to date, significant portions of the memo remain redacted in the newly released version, as well as, that doubts and questions about its legality persist.

20.4   See also

- Hepting v. AT&T (warrantless wiretapping case)

- MUSCULAR

- NSA call database

- NSA electronic surveillance program

- NSA warrantless surveillance controversy

- 2013 mass surveillance disclosures

- PRISM

20.5   References

[1] NSA Inspector General report on the President's Surveillance Program, March 24, 2009, page 10, note 3.

[2] "Is the FBI Up to the Job 10 Years After 9/11?" April 28, 2011

[3] Isikoff, Michael (December 13, 2008). "The Fed Who Blew the Whistle: Is he a hero or a criminal?". *Newsweek*. Archived from the original on December 15, 2008.

[4] Gellman, Barton (June 16, 2013). "U.S. surveillance architecture includes collection of revealing Internet, phone metadata". *The Washington Post*.

[5] Binney, William. *29C3 Panel: Jesselyn Radack, Thomas Drake, William Binney on whistleblowing and surveillance* (Flash) (YouTube Video). Hamburg, Germany: Chaos Communication Congress. Event occurs at 1:03:00. Retrieved June 9, 2013.

[6] Sanchez, Julian (July 29, 2013). "What the Ashcroft 'Hospital Showdown' on NSA spying was all about". Retrieved 2013-07-29.

[7] The New York Times, George W. Bush Made Retroactive N.S.A. 'Fix' After Hospital Room Showdown, September 20, 2015.

[8] Nakashima, Ellen (6 September 2014). "Legal memos released on Bush-era justification for warrantless wiretapping". Washington Post.

[9] Bamford, James (March 15, 2012). "The NSA Is Building the Country's Biggest Spy Center (Watch What You Say)". *Wired*. Retrieved March 15, 2012.

[10] "NSA inspector general report on email and internet data collection under Stellar Wind". March 9, 2009. Retrieved August 1, 2013.

[11] Savage, Charlie, Redactions in U.S. Memo Leave Doubts on Data Surveillance Program, The New York Times, Sunday, September 7, 2014, New York edition, page A17

20.6 External links

- NSA inspector general report on email and internet data collection under Stellar Wind – full document, The Guardian, June 27, 2013.

- Poitras, Laura. *The Program*. Nytimes.com, Op-Docs, August 22, 2012.

Chapter 21

Talx

TALX (pronounced talks) is now **Equifax Workforce Solutions**, a wholly owned subsidiary of Equifax.

21.1 History

Based out St. Louis, TALX was founded in 1973 as Interface Technology Inc. by several individuals including H. Richard "Rick" Grodsky, Professor of Electrical Engineering at Washington University. Interface Technology provided interactive voice response systems. Bill Canfield joined the company in 1986 as President and CEO in 1986 and added the title of Chairman in 1988. TALX went public listing on the NASDAQ in an IPO in 1996 and offered 2,000,000 shares at $9 per share for a total offer amount of $18,000,000. TALX Corp. At the time of the IPO, TALX designed and implemented interactive communication solutions using computer telephony to integrate technologies such as interactive voice response, facsimile, e-mail, Internet and corporate Intranet. TALX's interactive communication solutions enabled an organization's employees, customers, vendors and business partners to access, input and update information stored in data bases without human assistance. TALX also provided a branded employment and income verification service, The Work Number for Everyone, that a provided automated access to employment and salary records of large employers for purposes of loan and other credit approvals.

The events of September 11, 2001 caused TALX to shift its focus toward configurable data solutions and a recurring revenue model and away from custom on-premise software solutions. The employment and income verification service, The Work Number, as it was later became known, became the revenue and profit growth engine for the company. All future acquisitions and organic innovations were done to strengthen the employment and income verification business unit. March 2002 TALX Corporation acquired the two largest human resource outsourcing companies that specialized in unemployment cost management and related human resource applications, The Frick Company, the second largest provider headquartered in St. Louis, Missouri, and the largest provider of unemployment cost management business, Gates McDonald, a subsidiary of Nationwide Mutual Insurance Company, headquartered in Columbus, Ohio. [1] TALX sold it's e-Choice Benefits Enrollment Services business to Workscape in April 2003 to further focus on its core business of payroll-centric services with more standardized delivery platforms. [2]

During the period of 2002 and 2005, TALX increased its dominance in unemployment cost management services through acquisitions of Johnson & Associates LLC, TBT Enterprises Inc., UI Advantage Inc., Jon-Jay Associates Inc., Employers Unity Inc. and parts of Sheakley-Uniservice Inc. These acquisitions and the organic growth of The Work Number made TALX the dominate leader in employment and income verification and unemployment cost management services in the United States. TALX also added or created a number of other payroll-centric Human Resource related employer services including W-2 Management, I-9 Management, Tax Credit and Incentive Management, and Online Paperless Pay. TALX also successfully partnered with ADP, Ceridian, Aon-Hewitt and other payroll and benefit providers to package customized suites of services under several alliance banners.

In 2007, TALX was acquired by Equifax, one of the big three credit reporting agencies, in a transaction valued at $1.4 billion. [3] As of 2010, integration was completed and TALX now officially operates as a division of Equifax.

In October 2012, Equifax changed the name of the TALX business unit to Equifax Workforce Solutions to reflects the organization's commitment to leveraging its extensive workforce data with the analytics resources of Equifax.[4]

21.1.1 SEC Investigation of TALX

TALX disclosed in its July 2002 10-K filing that the Securities and Exchange Commission was conducting an investigation into its August 2001 secondary offering of common stock and second fiscal quarter 2001 financial results. TALX stated that they were cooperating fully with the investigation, and had voluntarily produced documents requested by the Commission and have made their employees available for interviews or testimony upon request. TALX stated that they believed that there is no basis for any action by the Commission. [5]

TALX reported in August 2004 that it has reached an agreement in principle with the staff of the Securities and Exchange Commission to settle its ongoing investigation of the company's accounting of certain items, which was the subject of the company's restatements of its 2001 and 2002 financial statements. Under the agreement in principle, the company would pay a fine of $2.5 million. Separately, William W. Canfield, the company's president and chief executive officer, reached an agreement in principle with the SEC staff to settle its ongoing investigation against him in a related matter. [6]

March 2005 TALX announced that the Securities and Exchange Commission (SEC) has accepted the previously announced offer of settlement submitted by TALX to resolve the SEC's investigation into its accounting for certain items. All financial statements in question have been previously restated to address the issues raised by the SEC. TALX agreed, without admitting or denying any liability, not to violate certain provisions of the Federal securities laws in the future. TALX also agreed to pay one dollar in disgorgement and $2.5 million in civil penalties. These amounts were paid into escrow by TALX in December 2004 and had been previously reflected in the company's financial statements. The SEC also accepted the offer of settlement submitted by William W. Canfield, TALX's president and chief executive officer, to resolve charges stemming from the same accounting issues. Canfield agreed, without admitting or denying any liability, not to violate certain provisions of the Federal securities laws in the future. He also agreed to pay $859,999 in disgorgement and $100,000 in civil penalties. [7]

The SEC filed fraud charges March 2005 against TALX Corp.'s former chief financial officer. The SEC alleged that Craig N. Cohen, who resigned in January 2004, violated antifraud and other federal securities laws by causing TALX to meet its 2001 financial target through fraudulent accounting practices. As a result, TALX overstated its 2001 income by about $2.1 million, or 65 percent, which inflated its stock price. Cohen then sold TALX shares. He is also accused of making misleading statements to auditors. The SEC sought a permanent injunction against Cohen, an officer and director bar and civil penalties. Cohen had served as chief financial officer from January 1994 to May 2003, and was vice president of application services and software from May 1999 to May 2003. He resigned at the same time TALX said it would restate its earnings for the fiscal years 1999 to 2003 to correct errors in the way it accounted for revenue. April 2007 the US District Court dismissed six of the seven counts against Cohen. The Court found Cohen guilty of the allegation of insufficient internal controls. The Court stated that there was evidence that Cohen knew he was falsely recording two projects as bill-an-hold transactions. The Court imposed a civil penalty against Cohen in the amount of $5,000.

21.1.2 FTC Investigation of TALX

June 2006 TALX announced that it was voluntarily responding to an initial inquiry by the Federal Trade Commission to assess whether TALX acquisitions in the unemployment compensation and Work Number businesses had significantly reduced competition. TALX believed it has complied with applicable regulatory filing requirements and intends to cooperate with the inquiry. [8]

The Federal Trade Commission announced April 2008 that it issued a complaint challenging a series of acquisitions by TALX Corporation that substantially lessened competition in the markets for outsourced unemployment compensation management (UCM) and verification of income and employment (VOIE) services. The Commission and TALX have reached an agreement settling the Commission's challenge. "TALX acted illegally," says Jeffrey Schmidt, Director of the FTC's Bureau of Competition, "by acquiring virtually all of its competition in a series of transactions. While each transaction individually may not have been problematic, the FTC looked at the cumulative effect of the acquisitions. This case sends a message that firms can't get away with unlawful acquisitions just because they take place in relatively small increments." The complaint alleges that TALX's acquisitions have enhanced its ability to increase prices unilaterally and to decrease the quality of services in the relevant markets. In addition, the complaint notes, TALX has alliance partners, including Automated Data Processing, Inc. (ADP), Convergys, Inc., and Ceridian, Inc., which have agreements with TALX to outsource to TALX some or all of the UCM services they provide for their clients.

According to the Commission, the relevant markets for outsourced VOIE and UCM services are highly concentrated, and TALX's acquisitions substantially increased concentration. The Commission alleges that entry into the relevant markets would not be timely, likely, or sufficient in magnitude, character, and scope to counteract the anticompetitive effects of the acquisitions. The complaint also alleges that entry and expansion in the outsourced UCM market for large, multi-state employers is made more difficult by the large number of customers tied to long-term contracts. Entry and expansion is also made more difficult by non-compete and non-solicitation agreements between TALX and its employees, which reduce the number of experienced persons available for hiring by potential competitors.

The proposed settlement, which is subject to final approval by the Commission following a 30-day public comment period, would foster market entry and expansion by current and future competitors. The settlement would allow long-term TALX customers to terminate their contracts and eliminate non-compete clauses for former and current TALX employees. [9]

21.1.3 Criticisms of TALX

In April 2010, The New York Times published an article about TALX. In short, TALX was accused of contesting unemployment benefits claims regardless of their merit in an effort to reduce the funds their clients—the employers—would have to pay to state unemployment insurance pools. The article pointed out that some unemployed persons were denied benefits as a result of TALX's actions. [10]

21.2 External links

- Official website

21.3 References

[1] http://investor.talx.com/phoenix.zhtml?c=74399&p=irol-newsArticle&ID=844530

[2] http://investor.talx.com/phoenix.zhtml?c=74399&p=irol-newsArticle&ID=403912

[3] http://investor.talx.com/phoenix.zhtml?c=74399&p=irol-newsArticle&ID=963591

[4] http://investor.equifax.com/releasedetail.cfm?ReleaseID=751150

[5] nvestor.talx.com/phoenix.zhtml?c=74399&p=irol-newsArticle&ID=311093

[6] http://investor.talx.com/phoenix.zhtml?c=74399&p=irol-newsArticle&ID=603790

[7] http://investor.talx.com/phoenix.zhtml?c=74399&p=irol-newsArticle&ID=681609

[8] http://investor.talx.com/phoenix.zhtml?c=74399&p=irol-newsArticle&ID=877336

[9] https://www.ftc.gov/news-events/press-releases/2008/04/ftc-challenges-acquisitions-talx-corp-stifled-competition

[10] http://www.nytimes.com/2010/04/04/us/04talx.html

Chapter 22

Zapaday

Zapaday is a global news calendar. The website publishes upcoming news headlines per day and per topic as a resource for journalists, bloggers, political analysts, marketers, event organisers, public relation professionals, scientists and travellers. Zapaday uses both bots and human editors to monitor over 4,000 news sites and calendars for future news stories, publishing its findings as news events on categorized calendars.

Users can create and publish their own events and calendars, re-using events and calendars of others for personal use.[2] On March 6, 2014, Zapaday launched a new subscription service with paid premium news calendars. The company also announced a new marketplace where journalists can syndicate curated news calendars as premium content.[3] The new model invites journalists and content creators to publish premium calendars and receive 50 per cent of earnings, while Zapaday will receive 20 per cent for hosting and handling. The remaining 30 per cent go to the seller, who can be either the content creator themselves, Zapaday, or one of the news agencies or other resellers that offer a white-label version of Zapaday to their clients.

Calendar events from Zapaday can be exported to a user's Outlook, Google Calendar, or a mobile phone at any time.[4]

Zapaday won an award as most promising start-up company across Europe at Tech Media Europe 2011[5] and was a 2012 Accenture Innovation Awards finalist.[6]

In December 2013, Zapaday, together with UK's GRNlive, the Foreign Correspondents Network, launched a new global reporting service where each future news event on Zapaday is accompanied with GRNlive journalists available in the region to cover the story on the ground.[7]

On 23 January 2013, Zapaday, together with Dutch press agency Algemeen Nederlands Persbureau (ANP), launched the renewed 'ANP Agenda' based on the Zapaday platform. The ANP Agenda includes planned domestic and sports news events, curated by ANP editors, and foreign and economic events curated by both ANP and Zapaday editors. Nearly 1.000 users from ANP, including journalists, broadcasters and communication professionals, now use the platform to spot upcoming news events and plan ahead.[8]

22.1   See also

- Reuters

- Algemeen Nederlands Persbureau

- Agence France-Presse

- Associated Press

- Recorded Future

22.2　References

[1] "Zapaday profile". Techcrunch. March 1, 2012.

[2] "About Zapaday section on Zapaday site". European Journalism Centre. October 5, 2011.

[3] "Zapaday launches Premium News Calendars, offers new Revenue Opportunity to Journalists" (PDF). March 6, 2014.

[4] "Zapaday – A Wiki-Style Events Calendar". Appvita. March 23, 2012.

[5] "Tech Media Europe Award for Zapaday". Illumy. February 3, 2011.

[6] "Zapaday, concept of the week and finalist: the news of tomorrow". Accenture. April 2012.

[7] "GRNlive and Zapaday launch news reporting network of the future" (PDF). Zapaday. December 19, 2013.

[8] (PDF) http://www.wan-ifra.org/system/files/.../20140123_ANP-Zapaday_finfin.pdf. Missing or empty |title= (help)

22.3　External links

- Official website

22.4 Text and image sources, contributors, and licenses

22.4.1 Text

- **Able Danger** *Source:* https://en.wikipedia.org/wiki/Able_Danger?oldid=680940392 *Contributors:* SimonP, Wichitalineman, Edward, Cimon Avaro, SEWilco, Etoile, Raul654, Jeffq, Phil Boswell, Tom harrison, TDC, Marcika, Mark5677, DragonflySixtyseven, Heirpixel, Commodore Sloat, Neutrality, Moverton, Rich Farmbrough, Pmsyyz, Jayc, Anonip, Clawson, Indio~enwiki, Arcadian, Uroshnor, Alansohn, Sherurcij, Geo Swan, Hipocrite, Calton, Gaytan, Katefan0, Ombudsman, Dominic, Sandover, Richard Arthur Norton (1958-), LOL, Tabletop, Striver, Mhoskins, Wayward, Matthew Platts, Rjwilmsi, Hiberniantears, Linuxbeak, Brighterorange, Yamamoto Ichiro, Ground Zero, AED, Stephan-Com, NekoDaemon, Physchim62, AlexP~enwiki, Tenebrae, Gaius Cornelius, Alex Bakharev, Pseudomonas, Brewthatistrue, Badagnani, Fosterremy, Dfgarcia, JPMcGrath, RonCram, GeoffCapp, Stinger296, Abrio, Sperril, Trilemma, Bhumiya, Blindjustice, Gorgonzilla, Arthur Rubin, Donald Albury, Mbarlotta, 0nslaught, Garybel, John Broughton, SmackBot, SQuast, JimmyCrackedCorn, Clpo13, Comp8956, Rmansour, SailorfromNH, Topdog08, TheKMan, Morton devonshire, Rangermike, John wesley, Voterrightsparty, Colinbartlett, NYCJosh, Fluppy, DabMachine, BranStark, Ericblazek, Eastlaw, Rupisis, CWY2190, Location, Untilzero, Huysman, Wikipediarules2221, Biruitorul, DulcetTone, DanTD, AntiVandalBot, Bigtimepeace, Spartaz, DuncanHill, Lan Di, Auric04, TAnthony, JBKramer, Ihafez, MetsBot, Torimar, Trusilver, Frank Freeman, Dispenser, Mcrawford01, ACBest, The Original Wildbear, Lvivske, PDFbot, Beasley Reece, Edkollin, DanaSaurSchloss, Thunderbird2, WereSpielChequers, Mhljones, The Evil Spartan, Anakin101, ClueBot, FieldMarine, Jeremiestrother, Tspooky, Michaeljburg, Jlray, DumZiBoT, F41rg4m3r, Kbdankbot, Addbot, Twhitmore.nz, StephenGraves, AbleDangerTheMovie, Evans1982, AnomieBOT, Raven1977, Mnnlaxer, Kithira, Abledanger6, Iqinn, Shanmugamp7, Trappist the monk, CorpusDei, RobertAllenWright, Ed11561, RjwilmsiBot, DASH-Bot, John of Reading, JohnCengiz77, Chire, H3llBot, Cmfowler3, 4thewin, Δ, Welhaven, Thewolfchild, Blufuss, ClueBot NG, Dufusrex, Mricha711, Widr, BG19bot, BattyBot, Stamptrader, A591A, Anisbests and Anonymous: 146

- **Anomaly Detection at Multiple Scales** *Source:* https://en.wikipedia.org/wiki/Anomaly_Detection_at_Multiple_Scales?oldid=674705511 *Contributors:* Disavian, Cydebot, LanceBarber, Tassedethe, AnomieBOT, VanishedUser sdu9aya9fasdsopa, John of Reading, Chire and Anonymous: 1

- **Behavioral analytics** *Source:* https://en.wikipedia.org/wiki/Behavioral_analytics?oldid=655186291 *Contributors:* Aubrew, McGeddon, Kuru, Keith D, Arjayay, Frze, Welthorpeedna, Cryptodd, Acetotyce, Photo.iep, Danieditor, NewsTeamAssemble, Howardmurraysobel and Anonymous: 3

- **Business analytics** *Source:* https://en.wikipedia.org/wiki/Business_analytics?oldid=689625512 *Contributors:* Michael Hardy, Kku, Michael Devore, Alvestrand, Gscshoyru, S.K., Mdd, Oleg Alexandrov, Mindmatrix, RHaworth, Rjwilmsi, Hans Genten, Random user 39849958, Rick lightburn, JLaTondre, XpXiXpY, SmackBot, Kuru, Cnbrb, Simonjohnpalmer, Earthlyreason, B, Alaibot, Vlado1, Vanished user ty12kl89jq10, Sarnalios~enwiki, Wcrosbie, Philip Trueman, Billinghurst, Kerenb, Emilygracedell, Fratrep, Melcombe, Founder DIPM Institute, Ukpremier, Tomas e, Jinij, Niceguyedc, Apparition11, Writerguy71, DeepOpinion, MrOllie, Crmguru2008, Citation bot, Emcien, FrescoBot, Rlistou, Boxplot, Pinethicket, I dream of horses, AmyDenise, Dnedzel, Full-date unlinking bot, Ethansdad, Trappist the monk, Crysb, Helwr, Timtempleton, Dries Debbaut, Chire, Idea Farm, Smithandteam, ClueBot NG, WhartonCAI, HMSSolent, Wbm1058, Singularit, Jamesx12345, Faizan, Picturepro, Huang cynthia, Photo.iep, Monkbot, Yashwantsnaik, Rasaxen, Olletove and Anonymous: 67

- **Cross Industry Standard Process for Data Mining** *Source:* https://en.wikipedia.org/wiki/Cross_Industry_Standard_Process_for_Data_Mining?oldid=676378512 *Contributors:* Kku, Kainaw, Woohookitty, Apayne, FlaBot, BMF81, AVM, Retired username, Gadget850, Smack-Bot, Cplakidas, Krexer, Ralf Klinkenberg, Gnome (Bot), MarshBot, Newsheep, Bissinger, Carmen56, EverGreg, Jamet123, Sunsetsky, Addbot, DOI bot, MrOllie, LaaknorBot, Yobot, USConsLib, Citation bot 1, Badmamajamer, Jackverr, Nigadk, Jesse V., EmausBot, Chire, EdoBot, Widr, Victorhache, BG19bot, Nancygrady, Deltahedron, Bradhill14, Kennethajensen, Ginsuloft, Monkbot, HelpUsStopSpam, Olavlaudy, Glenryman and Anonymous: 34

- **Customer analytics** *Source:* https://en.wikipedia.org/wiki/Customer_analytics?oldid=684724774 *Contributors:* Michael Hardy, Oleg Alexandrov, Malcolma, Kuru, Alaibot, Buxtonco, Risraelkloss, Mild Bill Hiccup, PixelBot, Addbot, Ben Ben, Yobot, FrescoBot, Groomtech, Boxplot, Kioumarsi, Mudx77, Wikipelli, Chire, MainFrame, Ralig, Jamesx12345, Blurrim, NewsTeamAssemble, Vidyasnap and Anonymous: 21

- **Data Applied** *Source:* https://en.wikipedia.org/wiki/Data_Applied?oldid=685577045 *Contributors:* DragonflySixtyseven, BD2412, Cydebot, Tnxman307, Download, Foobarnix, Crysb, Marksenizer, Chire and Anonymous: 3

- **Data mining in agriculture** *Source:* https://en.wikipedia.org/wiki/Data_mining_in_agriculture?oldid=642267706 *Contributors:* Michael Hardy, Tabletop, Hobit, SmackBot, Sean.hoyland, Mild Bill Hiccup, Niceguyedc, Qwfp, Forbes72, Drpickem, Yobot, AnomieBOT, FrescoBot, RjwilmsiBot, Chire, Toninowiki, Donner60, Gr650, ClueBot NG, Divine618 and Anonymous: 8

- **Data mining in meteorology** *Source:* https://en.wikipedia.org/wiki/Data_mining_in_meteorology?oldid=628896394 *Contributors:* Bearcat, Rjwilmsi, Pierre cb, Inks.LWC, Wilhelmina Will, EmausBot, AvicBot, Chire, Encycloshave, Mr Sheep Measham, Helpful Pixie Bot, Inoshika, BattyBot, Mohamed-Ahmed-FG and Anonymous: 4

- **Educational data mining** *Source:* https://en.wikipedia.org/wiki/Educational_data_mining?oldid=686542707 *Contributors:* Tabletop, Qwertyus, Rjwilmsi, Turadg, Neiltheffernaniii, Cydebot, DumbBOT, Kudpung, Katharineamy, Malcolmxl5, Melcombe, Arjayay, Boleyn, Yobot, Nsisim, AnomieBOT, Sventura, Tbhotch, Jesse V., Mean as custard, Dewritech, Chire, Morgankevinj AWB, Delusion23, Helpful Pixie Bot, Wbm1058, Uksas, In1romoc, Jamesmcmahon0, Fgegypt, Mengqian Gu, Segedyjr, Monkbot, Mabelho, TC EDM, Anshurm, Jpchibole, N.kandoi and Anonymous: 15

- **Examples of data mining** *Source:* https://en.wikipedia.org/wiki/Examples_of_data_mining?oldid=685575767 *Contributors:* Ost316, Chire and Vemula95

- **Human genetic clustering** *Source:* https://en.wikipedia.org/wiki/Human_genetic_clustering?oldid=685428282 *Contributors:* Michael Hardy, Bearcat, Woohookitty, Rjwilmsi, Carwil, Wobble, Bgwhite, Muntuwandi, SmackBot, Chris the speller, Doug Weller, Simul, Guy Macon, Professor marginalia, David Eppstein, Mange01, Flyer22 Reborn, Aprock, ThVa, Atethnekos, Vyom25, Middayexpress, Yobot, AnomieBOT, Maulucioni, Moxy, Saul Greenberg, Jjberg2, Victorius III, Laofmoonster, Gwicky, Koozedine, Millstoner, Semmler, Tijfo098, Miradre, Maklinovich, Helpful Pixie Bot, BG19bot, ArtifexMayhem, Go ahead punk, Axel Stone, ChrisGualtieri, FonsScientiae, Monkbot, Truthgod666 and Anonymous: 9

- **Inference attack** *Source:* https://en.wikipedia.org/wiki/Inference_attack?oldid=633792158 *Contributors:* Centrx, Bachrach44, Xaosflux, Alaibot, Contextflexed, S79sut, Addbot, Emil Bild, PigFlu Oink, DrilBot, Chire, RimuDas and Anonymous: 2

- **Java Data Mining** *Source:* https://en.wikipedia.org/wiki/Java_Data_Mining?oldid=646774576 *Contributors:* Ronz, Khalid hassani, Neilc, John Vandenberg, Stardust8212, Sango123, BOT-Superzerocool, Sergio.ballestrero, GRuban, Doug Bell, Ralf Klinkenberg, VoABot II, Mnt, Sunil v74, Mark.hornick, Billinghurst, John baba1, Dank, Addbot, Yobot, Ptbotgourou, FrescoBot, Helwr, Chire and Anonymous: 15

- **Open-source intelligence** *Source:* https://en.wikipedia.org/wiki/Open-source_intelligence?oldid=685847728 *Contributors:* Bryan Derksen, Edward, Nealmcb, Isomorphic, Tregoweth, Ronz, Theresa knott, Kaihsu, Katana0182, Topbanana, Drxenocide, Nurg, Stewartadcock, Michael Snow, Mattflaschen, Ancheta Wis, DocWatson42, Rj, Finn-Zoltan, Mboverload, Pascal666, Khalid hassani, Neilc, Fuck you Very Much, Beland, Loremaster, Klemen Kocjancic, Kevyn, Ta bu shi da yu, Discospinster, Guanabot, Pmsyyz, Jnestorius, Causa sui, Townmouse, Silver hr, Calton, Velella, RHaworth, Apokrif, SCEhardt, Stefanomione, Xenoncloud, Rjwilmsi, Jhballard, YurikBot, Infos~enwiki, Filippof, Longbow4u, RobWeir, Ansell, Oenomel, Tony1, Deku-shrub, Mendicott, WAS 4.250, Sandstein, Arthur Rubin, Tierce, GrinBot~enwiki, SmackBot, Zhopa, Mdd4696, Ckras, Mauls, Master Jay, Bluebot, Thumperward, StrangerInParadise, Antonrojo, Frap, Engwar, Gamgee, ALR, Ligulembot, Dave314159, Jacopo, Isria, TastyPoutine, Mhpolak, JoeBot, ComLinks, JForget, CmdrObot, Ninetyone, CWY2190, Timtrent, Zeroeffect, Cydebot, Fl, Dancter, Thijs!bot, Hcberkowitz, JustAGal, OSINT, WilsonjrWikipedia, Alphachimpbot, Bear@oss.net, Erxnmedia, Robert Steele, Quenca, OSC Flunkee, LouieLobo, Scolbath, O'Mara, R'n'B, JPLeonard, Webconomist, STBotD, Stanqo, AzureCitizen, Creche, VolkovBot, Jeff G., JhsBot, LanceBarber, Rworden, SieBot, Desertson, Yintan, Toddst1, Axiomatica, Bugcatchers, ClueBot, Lawrence Cohen, Laudak, Particle010, Leo Fitzpatrick, Gwguffey, Rhododendrites, Aurora2698, Tnxman307, Yankee white, Victor McGuire, XLinkBot, SilvonenBot, Plausible to deny, RobertDavidSteeleVivas, Addbot, Jafeluv, Br1z, Lightbot, Jarble, חובבשירה, AnomieBOT, VanishedUser sdu9aya9fasdsopa, Bear bs, Xqbot, Nasa-verve, GrouchoBot, FrescoBot, Writer76116, Full-date unlinking bot, Moshe2009, Buddy23Lee, Lotje, Jensj17, Dpscargill, Lkedia11, Eddieshrop, RA0808, Get A Trip, ZéroBot, Chire, JoeSperrazza, HeLmiT, ClueBot NG, Israelvonrurach, OSICEurope, Jeff Song, Widr, Barely3am, Shirudo, Dannyruthe, Mrufianspain, Federicooran, Nfiorentino, Bmw745li2003 and Anonymous: 130

- **Path analysis (computing)** *Source:* https://en.wikipedia.org/wiki/Path_analysis_(computing)?oldid=637394374 *Contributors:* Lgallindo, Graham87, Tesler, Alynna Kasmira, Black Falcon, Tom Morris, SmackBot, McGeddon, Kuru, Alaibot, Bonadea, Janahan, ImageRemovalBot, Jonathan Oldenbuck, Tijnonline, Addbot, Locobot, PieceOfNut, Veddit, Welthorpeedna, BattyBot, DoctorKubla, Photo.iep, Howardmurraysobel and Anonymous: 6

- **Police-enforced ANPR in the UK** *Source:* https://en.wikipedia.org/wiki/Police-enforced_ANPR_in_the_UK?oldid=687127776 *Contributors:* William Avery, Michael Hardy, Gabbe, Dale Arnett, Smjg, Rich Farmbrough, MisterSheik, Andrew Gray, Henry W. Schmitt, Woohookitty, BD2412, Gareth E Kegg, Wavelength, Neilbeach, Kingboyk, SmackBot, DOuG, Stifle, Mauls, Chendy, ALR, Warniats, Whisperwolf, Ninetyone, Cydebot, Mattisse, SGGH, Smartse, Robina Fox, Keith D, AtholM, Cometstyles, Jevansen, 386-DX, Mwilso24, Feudonym, Orthorhombic, Quoth nevermore~enwiki, Elassint, Rumping, Joe sav4, Yobot, LilHelpa, Thinkblueskies, FrescoBot, Leboite, Full-date unlinking bot, Jonkerz, Connelly90, RjwilmsiBot, GoingBatty, Chire, 1234r00t, Carmichael, PhnomPencil, MarchOrDie, Whizz40 and Anonymous: 37

- **Proactive Discovery of Insider Threats Using Graph Analysis and Learning** *Source:* https://en.wikipedia.org/wiki/Proactive_Discovery_of_Insider_Threats_Using_Graph_Analysis_and_Learning?oldid=674705663 *Contributors:* Disavian, Cydebot, PamD, Ktr101, AnomieBOT, VanishedUser sdu9aya9fasdsopa, GoingBatty and Anonymous: 2

- **SEMMA** *Source:* https://en.wikipedia.org/wiki/SEMMA?oldid=671407254 *Contributors:* Gadget850, Krexer, Martijn Hoekstra, Addbot, Yobot, FrescoBot, Lotje, John of Reading, NodBot, Fularp, Chadills75 and Anonymous: 7

- **Stellar Wind** *Source:* https://en.wikipedia.org/wiki/Stellar_Wind?oldid=683970712 *Contributors:* WhisperToMe, Rpyle731, Evolauxia, Cuchullain, Ground Zero, Jsheehy, Hydrargyrum, Malcolma, Johnpseudo, SmackBot, Verne Equinox, Fintler, Colonies Chris, Ohconfucius, Byelf2007, HelloAnnyong, ToastyMallows, Woodshed, Gnurkel, Widefox, Albany NY, Stinkyasp, RockMFR, 83d40m, Ask123, Edkollin, Arbor to SJ, Dillard421, Hamiltondaniel, Kai-Hendrik, Debresser, Blaylockjam10, Tassedethe, Mps, DrFleischman, VanishedUser sdu9aya9fasdsopa, LilHelpa, Matttoothman, Whistlepunk, Puppier, Enemenemu, Noloader, Billt568, Thargor Orlando, Chire, Brycehughes, Xanchester, ClueBot NG, Kendall-K1, A1candidate, BattyBot, Cloudsaboveus, P3Y229, Jackpots777, Badwool87, P2Peter, Someone not using his real name, Paulmd199, Wilson945, Je.est.un.autre, Thewhitebox and Anonymous: 13

- **Talx** *Source:* https://en.wikipedia.org/wiki/Talx?oldid=680402253 *Contributors:* Chaser, SmackBot, GoldDragon, Shortride, Jboarman, Jeanneachille, Santryl, Regancy42, John of Reading, Chire, BardamuNJ10, ClueBot NG, Danim, Daveed84x, Destroyedtalx, Wmson120 and Anonymous: 6

- **Zapaday** *Source:* https://en.wikipedia.org/wiki/Zapaday?oldid=688766425 *Contributors:* Bearcat, Gidonb, Grutness, Cydebot, Dawkeye, Magioladitis, Havanafreestone, Jorgath, SchreiberBike, Yobot, Ivanvector, Editør, BattyBot, ChrisGualtieri, Yash!, 7Sidz and Anonymous: 4

22.4.2 Images

- **File:2010-05-14-USCYBERCOM_Logo.jpg** *Source:* https://upload.wikimedia.org/wikipedia/commons/3/3a/2010-05-14-USCYBERCOM_Logo.jpg *License:* Public domain *Contributors:* Department of Defense *Original artist:* http://www.defense.gov/home/features/2010/0410_cybersec/images/cybercom_seal_large1.jpg Department of Defense

- **File:Ambox_globe_content.svg** *Source:* https://upload.wikimedia.org/wikipedia/commons/b/bd/Ambox_globe_content.svg *License:* Public domain *Contributors:* Own work, using File:Information icon3.svg and File:Earth clip art.svg *Original artist:* penubag

- **File:Boundless_Informant_data_collection.svg** *Source:* https://upload.wikimedia.org/wikipedia/commons/5/5b/Boundless_Informant_data_collection.svg *License:* CC0 *Contributors:* BlankMap-World6.svg
Original artist: Rezonansowy

- **File:CIA.svg** *Source:* https://upload.wikimedia.org/wikipedia/commons/2/23/CIA.svg *License:* Public domain *Contributors:* http://www.law.cornell.edu/uscode/50/403m.html *Original artist:* United States federal government

22.4.3   Content license